The New Eurocrats

National Civil Servants in EU Policy-making

Karin Geuijen

Paul 't Hart

Sebastiaan Princen

Kutsal Yesilkagit

AMSTERDAM UNIVERSITY PRESS

Cover design: Maedium, Utrecht
Layout: Het Steen Typografie, Maarssen

ISBN 978 90 5356 797 5
NUR 754

CONTENTS

Tables and Figures   8

Acknowledgements   11

CHAPTER ONE:
STUDYING EUROCRATS AT WORK   13

1.1   Emerging Eurocracy: National civil servants and European
      integration   13
1.2   From diplomats to international experts   15
1.3   Tensions and dilemmas in diplomatic practice   21
1.4   Research questions   23
1.5   Methods   24
1.6   Book plan   27

CHAPTER TWO:
TOWARD A EUROPEANISED CIVIL SERVICE?
A SURVEY STUDY   31

2.1   Surveying the Dutch civil service   31
2.2   Finding Dutch 'Eurocrats'   33
2.3   The organisational context of Dutch Eurocracy   41
2.4   The virtuous spiral of organisational Europeanisation   48

CHAPTER THREE:
EUROCRATIC WORK AS STRATEGIC BEHAVIOUR: MOVING
BEFORE THE COMMISSION DOES IN VETERINARY POLICY   51

3.1   Representing the 'national interest' in Brussels   51
3.2   Uploading in the pre-proposal phase   52
3.3   Research design   57
3.4   Frontloading, signalling and coalition formation in veterinary
      policy   58
3.5   Eurocratic work as strategic behaviour: Conclusions   73

CHAPTER FOUR:
GETTING THINGS DONE IN EUROPEAN POLICE
CO-OPERATION   77

4.1   Eurocratic work in the Third Pillar: A different world?   77
4.2   The case of data availability: 'Messy' policy-making in Europe   78
4.3   Species of Eurocrats   85
4.4   Understanding national Eurocrats: Conclusions   99

CHAPTER FIVE:
BRIDGE BUILDERS OR BRIDGEHEADS IN BRUSSELS?
THE WORLD OF SECONDED NATIONAL EXPERTS   103

5.1   Living and breathing the Brussels bureaucracy   103
5.2   Getting inside the insiders: Methodology and data   105
5.3   Demand and supply: The Dutch and the expert secondment
      system   106
5.4   Profiling the Dutch expert contingent   111
5.5   Knowing how and knowing who: Networking   113
5.6   Life after secondment: SNEs and their careers   123
5.7   An underutilised asset: Conclusions   125

CHAPTER SIX:
UNDERSTANDING EUROCRATIC WORK:
CONCLUSIONS AND REFLECTIONS   129

6.1   Dutch Eurocracy revisited   129
6.2   Eurocrats: How many, where?   130
6.3   Eurocratic work: Individual professionalism   131
6.4   Eurocratic work: Organisational preconditions   140
6.5   Grasping the real world of Eurocracy: The road ahead   146

Appendix   151

Notes   153

Bibliography   161

About the authors   171

Index   173

TABLES AND FIGURES

TABLES

Table 1.1	Two models of diplomatic representation	18
Table 2.1	EU involvement among civil servants	33
Table 2.2	EU involvement by job type	35
Table 2.3	EU involvement by educational level	35
Table 2.4	Time share of EU-related work among civil servants whose work is affected by the EU	37
Table 2.5	Importance of specific EU-related activities among civil servants whose work is affected by the EU	38
Table 2.6	Factor loading of the specific EU-related activities on the two extracted components	39
Table 2.7	Cross-table between 'Importance of participation in Council Working Groups' and 'Importance of participation in Commission Working Groups'	40
Table 2.8	EU involvement, median time spent and dispersion index by government organisation	43
Table 2.9	Overall responses to the six statements	46
Table 2.10	Responses to the six statements by respondents in the three types of organisations	47
Table 4.1	Dutch Eurocrats: Three ideal types	100
Table 5.1	Commission Directorate-Generals as SNE Receivers	108
Table 5.2	Dutch ministries and agencies as SNE Providers	110
Table 5.3	Ranks of Dutch SNEs at the time of secondment	112
Table 5.4	Frequency of Dutch SNE contacts	115

Table 5.5   SNE return rate after secondment   125

Table 6.1   Strengths and weaknesses of Eurocratic ideal types   132

FIGURES:

Figure 2.1. Time spent on EU-related activities by civil servants
           whose work is affected by the EU   36

ACKNOWLEDGEMENTS

The researchers would like to thank a number of people for their support during the process of doing this study. First, we would like to thank the Dutch Ministry of the Interior (BZK) for its financial support and the members of the supervisory group for their comments and suggestions during our discussions in The Hague. We would like to extend our particular thanks to Tanja Timmermans, who was our contact at the Ministry and helped us contact the right people on several occasions, and to Daphne de Groot, who took over this role during the final stages of the process.

We would like to thank André Dickmann for his generous offer to include a number of questions in the large-scale POMO survey that he coordinated for the Ministry of the Interior. Moreover, his expertise was of great help in further developing the survey questions and analysing the survey data. Melchior Bus opened doors to EU co-ordinators in various ministries to identify and contact potential participants for the expert meetings we held. Commissioner Anita Hazenberg generously provided us with an extensive briefing about who is who in the Dutch community of policemen and policy bureaucrats working on European police co-operation. Guido van Os offered much needed assistance in transcribing the expert meeting discussions.

Drafts of some of the chapters of this report were commented on by fellow scholars. In particular, we would like to thank Mirko Noordegraaf (Utrecht University), Rod Rhodes (Australian National University), Dvora Yanow (VU University of Amsterdam) and Jane Mansbridge (Harvard University) for useful feedback and advice.

Finally, our thanks go out to all those people who, either as interviewees or as participants in the expert meetings, were willing to share their experiences and ideas with us. In particular, we would like to thank the people who allowed us to 'shadow' them in the hallways and meeting rooms of The

Hague, Brussels and elsewhere as they went about their Eurocratic working days. These interviews and observation periods have been invaluable.

This study was conceived and conducted by the four of us. However, three other individuals have made crucial contributions to parts of it. Our co-author on chapter 3 was Ellen Mastenbroek of Radboud University, Nijmegen. And chapter 5 was written entirely by Semin Suvarierol of Utrecht University and Caspar van den Berg of Leiden University as a standalone project which fitted into the overall framework of this study perfectly and its findings are therefore included in this book. We are grateful for their pivotal contributions to this book.

Karin Geuijen, Paul 't Hart, Sebastiaan Princen, Kutsal Yesilkagit
Utrecht and Canberra, November 2007

CHAPTER 1

STUDYING EUROCRATS AT WORK

1.1 Emerging Eurocracy: National civil servants and European integration

Civil servants from the various European Union (EU) member states are among the most ubiquitous and important players in European governance. Within the formal EU structures, they are involved in a myriad of Commission expert groups, Council working parties, and 'comitology' committees, as well as a range of advisory committees. In these various groups and committees, their roles vary from preparing decisions and giving advice to approving proposals on behalf of their political superiors and taking or implementing decisions. In addition, civil servants are active outside of these formal EU-related structures, either in independent networks of officials and regulators or in ad hoc contacts with their counterparts in other countries.

Together, these civil servants form a dense web of what Slaughter (2004) has called 'government networks'. In her study of government networks, Slaughter showed the vast array of functions they perform in terms of exchanging information, co-ordinating the enforcement of regulations, and harmonising national regulations when those regulations have effects across borders. According to Slaughter, the rise of government networks is indicative of a 'new world order', in which states no longer present themselves on the international scene as unitary actors, speaking and acting with one voice, but rather as disaggregated states in which functionally specialised parts of government directly interact with their counterparts in other countries.

Despite the importance of civil servants in international and EU governance, relatively little is known about who they are and what they do. National civil servants take centre stage in three strands of literature. The best known of these strands is the literature on the national co-ordination of EU policies (cf. Harmsen 1999; Kassim et al. 2000; Peters and Wright 2000).

The central concern of these studies is how the domestic administrations of EU member states co-ordinate internally in order to produce a 'national position' in Brussels. Given this specific concern, this literature pays less attention to what civil servants actually do when they go to Brussels. Second, a group focused on Scandinavian scholars has conducted a number of surveys among domestic civil servants. Some of these surveys seek to establish the importance of EU-related work within the civil service at large (Egeberg and Trondal 1999; Lægreid et al. 2004), while others focus more specifically on the role conceptions of civil servants who are active in committees and working groups of the European Commission and the Council of Ministers (Beyers 2005; Beyers and Trondal 2004; Egeberg 1999; Trondal 2002; Trondal and Veggeland 2003). Finally, a few isolated studies have followed the activities of national civil servants in EU venues firsthand through in-depth case studies and observation (Thedvall 2006; 2007).

These literatures offer parts of the picture, but overall they pale in comparison to the vast amounts of literature that analyse the more visible 'political' aspects of EU policy-making, including the negotiations over major treaty changes and the political processes that take place within and between the EU's institutions in formal decision-making. As part of these processes, national civil servants sometimes pop up as the actors who prepare or implement a decision. Nevertheless, their role in the process tends to remain a black box. National civil servants are part of the 'unseen hand' in European governance, which also comprises Commission officials, companies, lobbyists, and secretaries of the Council (Van Schendelen and Scully 2003).

In this book, we seek to open the black box and shed light on this 'hidden world' of EU governance by studying the role of national civil servants in EU governance. We will call them 'national Eurocrats' throughout this study. We study them by systematically examining civil servants from one member state: the Netherlands.[1] In doing so, we seek to add to – and integrate – two of the studies mentioned above: the existing surveys among civil servants in Scandinavian countries, and the emerging literature on the activities of national civil servants in the EU's daily policy-making processes. Through a combination of quantitative and qualitative research methods, we highlight the extent of civil servant involvement in processes of EU governance as well as the specific activities they perform and the roles they play within these processes. We will use the remainder of this chapter to sketch the theoretical background to this study, formulate more precisely the questions to be answered, detail and justify the methods used to answer them, and draw the outlines of the subsequent empirical chapters.

1.2 From diplomats to international experts

The wide involvement of national civil servants in EU policy-making processes is indicative of a broader trend in the way the international representation of states is organised. In ideal-typical terms, it signifies a move away from the 'classic' model of diplomacy carried out by a unified diplomatic service. This model draws a clear line between international representation and other areas of government policy. International representation is conducted by professional diplomats, who claim to have the specific expertise needed to deal with the diplomats of other states. Other civil servants deal with domestic affairs, and insofar as these 'domestic' policies have an international dimension, this external dimension is again the responsibility of professional diplomats. For example, in this model, environmental specialists develop domestic environmental policies, but diplomats carry out negotiations on international environmental agreements. Moreover, the diplomatic service is highly formalised and hierarchical, with clear channels of command and accountability. This allows governments to exert a high degree of control over their external relations and to maintain a 'single voice' toward other governments.

In the alternative model, which is exemplified by Slaughter's analysis of government networks, international relations are carried out by a multitude of civil servants, each of whom deal with their own area of expertise. Not only do environmental civil servants develop domestic policies but they also conduct international talks and negotiations on these topics. Taken to its extreme, this implies the absence of a single chain of hierarchy in the international field. There may be hierarchical relations within a policy area, but there is no one overarching formal structure of hierarchical accountability and control in international affairs. Thus, in this model, governments 'dissolve' in their constituent components and maintain a multitude of (independent) ties with their counterparts in other governments.

This underlying shift in the form and organisation of diplomacy is important for understanding the background to and results of this study. Therefore, we will first discuss in greater detail what the crucial assumptions are that underlie the two models and to what extent the shift from the classic to the new model has been documented in the literature. This provides the background to the subsequent discussion of the tensions and dilemmas inherent in the practices of domestic civil servants in EU governance, which inform the central questions of this study.

Two models of international representation
The classic model of international diplomacy evolved from the 17th century onwards and had three defining characteristics (cf. Coolsaet 1998: 3; see also Melissen 2006). First, diplomacy was considered to be a specific profession, apart from policy-specific or 'technical' expertise. This premise was derived from 'the notion that all the most important foreign policy decisions were essentially political, and that the skills required to handle them were derived from intuition and experience' (Hamilton and Langhorne 1995: 218). In terms of organising a country's diplomatic service, this implied that diplomacy was meant to be a lifetime career, and that each diplomat had to enter the service at the lowest level (Kennan 1997: 200). Second, diplomats operated within a centralised organisation led by a Ministry of Foreign Affairs. This system allowed information from different sources to be processed in one place, thus ensuring a consistent voice in the state's external relations. Third, the diplomatic model took bilateral relations between states as its foundation.

The classic model was built on a conception of the state as a single unit. A diplomat was supposed to be 'speaking for the supreme source of power in his own country' (Kennan 1997: 204). Moreover, foreign policy and domestic policy were supposed to be completely separate. Foreign policy focused on 'the double agenda of diplomacy for centuries: commercial issues and security' (Coolsaet 1998: 4). Insofar as international commitments impinged on domestic policies, it was assumed that 'some single coherent and responsible centre of power [the supreme power in the quote above] (...) was in a position to compel the country's other authorities to play their part in meeting any commitments made through the diplomatic process' (Kennan 1997: 204).

The classic model in its pure form has always been subject to challenges (Craig, George and Lauren 2006). In the literature, these challenges have been explained with reference to two developments: the growing scope and complexity of the international policy agenda and the rise of multilateralism. The growing international policy agenda has led to a tension between the conception of diplomacy as a distinct, 'non-technical' profession and the need for specialised policy-specific knowledge to deal with issues of a highly technical nature. This tension has run parallel with the blurring between foreign policy and domestic policy. In the years between and directly after the two world wars, the main challenge to traditional diplomacy came from economists, who were placed in embassies to deal with the growing importance of international economic policy co-ordination (Hamilton and Langhorne 1995: 169-170 and 203-204). Since then, the international agenda has come to encompass a wide range of issues that in earlier times were thought to be domestic in scope, such as environmental policy, social policy and health policy. This has undermined one of the basic assumptions underlying the diplomatic model, that is, the separation between foreign and domestic policy. Furthermore, it has led to a proliferation of direct contacts between policy-specific departments in different countries, which Berridge (2002: 15) has described as 'direct-dial diplomacy'.

Other authors (e.g., Coolsaet 1998) identify the rise of multilateralism as the driving force behind the rise of a new type of diplomat. Since multilateral forums typically deal with specific issues, countries tend to staff them with specialists in those areas who, moreover, often report directly to a policy-specific department rather than the Ministry of Foreign Affairs (Kennan 1997: 207). Nowhere is this trend clearer than in the EU, which has established a plethora of specific forums to deal with almost every conceivable policy area.

This way of organising a country's international representation can be seen as a shift toward a new model of international representation. In its purest form, this model has quite a different set of characteristics than the classic model. To begin with, international representation is seen as an integral part of a policy area, and the main claim to professional knowledge is related to substantive technical expertise rather than diplomatic expertise. As a result, a country is represented by environmental civil servants in talks and negotiations on international environmental policies or by criminal justice experts in international crime policies. Second, the government's external representation is not organised in a single hierarchical system. There is no single 'foreign office' that co-ordinates all of the external relations. Rather, governmental representatives report directly to their 'own' department and have little to do with representatives from other departments. Insofar as co-ordination among them takes place, this only occurs through the mechanisms that are available for domestic policy co-ordination, not through the Ministry of Foreign Affairs. As Coolsaet (1998: 21) notes, this development 'gives the current diplomatic structure and organisation a cobweb character, without main threads as it seems'. Finally, the new model is not primarily based on bilateral diplomatic relations but on a combination of bilateral and multilateral relations, in which the emphasis often lies on the latter.

In terms of underlying assumptions, the new model of diplomacy also stands diametrically opposed to the classic model. The state is not seen as a single unit embodied by a 'supreme power', but as a collection of government agencies. In Slaughter's words, the state has become a 'disaggregated state'; disaggregated, that is, 'into its component institutions', which maintain a multitude of ties with their counterparts in other countries (Slaughter 2000: 178; 2004: 12-15). As a corollary, as was already explained above, the new model in its pure form does not assume a distinction between foreign policy and domestic policy, but treats these as two components of a given policy area. An overview of the characteristics of and assumptions underlying the two models of diplomatic representation is presented in table 1.1.

	Classic model	New model
Characteristics:		
Role of diplomatic professionalism	Diplomacy as a distinct profession	Diplomacy as aspect of policy-specific professionalism
Organisation of diplomatic service	Hierarchical in a Ministry of Foreign Affairs	Non-hierarchical, reporting to specialised departments
Main type of diplomatic relations	Bilateral	Bilateral and multilateral
Assumptions:		
Nature of the state	Single unit with sovereign power	Multitude of government agencies with functional specialisations
Distinction between foreign policy and domestic policy	Clear separation between foreign and domestic policy	No separation between foreign and domestic policy

Table 1.1 *Two models of diplomatic representation*

Towards a new model of diplomacy?

These two models are extremes, 'ideal types', which in their pure form have never existed in reality. Still, in recent decades the new model seems to have become more important relative to the classic model, because of the widening scope of issues that are discussed at the international level and the increased levels of specialised knowledge that are required to deal with these issues in international (often multilateral) forums.

These shifts have been widely documented in the literature on diplomacy and international relations. For instance, Berridge (2002: 14) notes that 'it is rare for [a Ministry of Foreign Affairs] now to have the same authority in the conduct of foreign relations relative to other ministries that it once had' and 'in all states the "line ministries" – trade, finance, defence, transport, environment and so on (...) – now engage in direct communication not only with their foreign counterparts but also with quite different agencies abroad'. On a similar note, Hamilton and Langhorne (1995: 217) claim that 'diplomatic inflation has tended (...) to modify the role of the professional generalist. The pace of technological change, the speed of modern communications, and a heightened awareness of regional and global interdependence, have meant increased involvement in external affairs by domestic ministries'. For Coolsaet (1998: 18), 'the declining role of the Ministry of Foreign Affairs as the central channel for diplomatic relations with other states' is 'a central characteristic' of the way states have adapted to the rise of multilateral forums.

It is more difficult to pinpoint the shift between the two models in quantitative terms, but some figures exist. In 1997, George Kennan (1997: 206) estimated that approximately 70 % of all US diplomatic mission personnel came from other departments and agencies than the US Department of State. The relative importance of these departments and agencies also varies over time. For instance, between 1986 and 1996, the number of employees from the US Departments of Health, Justice and Transportation in foreign US missions increased dramatically, while the number of the US Agency for International Development, Department of Agriculture and US Information Agency employees declined (Talbott 1997).

The most fertile ground for these new forms of diplomacy is the European Union – both because its remit extends to a wide range of policy issues and because it is the world's strongest supranational organisation. Under the aegis of the EU, thousands of national civil servants meet regularly in a wide range of committees and working groups to discuss and decide on European policies and regulatory standards. The exact number of the Commission's expert groups, 'comitology' committees and the Council's working parties is difficult to assess, since some groups may be dormant while others do not appear in official overviews. Wessels and Rometsch (1996: 331) estimate that approximately 25,000 national officials were involved in Council and Commission working groups in 1994. Drawing on a Commission overview from 2004, Brandsma (2006) counted some 1,090 expert groups, excluding subgroups and working groups within these expert groups. Moreover, the number of Council working parties is estimated at some 160, while the number of 'comitology' committees, in which member state representatives monitor the implementation of EU law by the European Commission, stands at approximately 320. Most of these groups are typically attended by lower-ranking civil servants who are specialists in their policy field or on a specific policy issue. In addition to departmental civil servants, these groups may also include representatives from independent agencies in the member states.

The most systematic data on participation in EU policy-making by domestic civil servants can be found in surveys conducted in the Nordic countries. In a survey among officials from ministries and directorates in Norway, not even an EU member state, approximately 45% of respondents (both in ministries and in directorates) indicated that they were affected 'to some extent or more' by the EU and/or the EEA Agreement (to which Norway is a party). In the Ministry of Foreign Affairs, this was as high as 61% (Egeberg and Trondal 1999: 135). Although the impact does not imply that an official is active within the EU, the figure does attest to the importance of the EU for domestic civil servants.

In a survey among governmental units in Norway, Iceland, Sweden and Finland (two EU members and two non-members), Lægreid et al. (2004) report figures concerning the perceived impact of the EU and the countries' contacts with EU institutions and their participation in EU committees. The number of respondents who perceive 'the overall consequences of EU/EEA policies and regulations on their department' to be 'fairly large/ very large' ranges between 31% (for Norway) and 64% (for Iceland), with 57% for both Sweden and Finland. In terms of actual contacts, their results show that most of their contacts are with the Commission (a high of 43% of respondents in Sweden), while participation in EU committees ranges from between 7% (for comitology committees among Finnish respondents) and 26% (for Commission expert committees, again among Finnish respondents). These figures probably overestimate the levels of contact since the survey was conducted among the 'EU specialists' of each governmental unit. Still, they indicate the wide range of officials within those countries' governments who are active in EU policy-making.

1.3 Tensions and dilemmas in diplomatic practice

Despite the rise of the new model of diplomacy, elements of both models can be identified in the international representation of most states. The new model presents itself most clearly in terms of the multitude of specialised civil servants participating in working groups, expert groups and other types of committees in the EU and other international organisations, as well as in their direct links with counterparts in other countries.

The classic model is present in the attempts at co-ordinating the national input in international forums. This is exemplified by the central co-ordinating role that Ministries of Foreign Affairs formally play in their states' international policies (Hocking and Spence 2002). At embassies, the officials from specialised departments operate under the aegis of an ambassador who has most likely made the diplomatic services his or her career. These elements of formalisation and hierarchy based on the classic model serve to guarantee at least some unity of voice in international arenas, predicated on the idea that there is an overarching 'national interest' which supersedes the specific interests that may exist in the various policy areas.

This duality in international representation does create some tension. Looked at from the classic model, parallel and non-hierarchical representation may easily lead to a lack of accountability, unwanted and unforeseen commitments, and contradictory inputs that may weaken the overall effectiveness of a country in the international arena. Looked at from the viewpoint of the new model, formalisation and hierarchy lead to inflexibility and a loss of expertise that, in turn, will undermine the effectiveness of the government's activities in international affairs.

This tension becomes most visible at the level of the individuals representing a government in an international forum or vis-à-vis their counterparts in another country. In the end, it is at the individual level that choices are made and organisational arrangements are put into practice. Thus, a central claim of our study is that a focus on individuals will help us to learn more about the way the diplomatic representation of various governments presently operates.

Moreover, new forms of diplomacy suffer from dilemmas that were also present in the classic model of diplomacy but the classic model had at least found some solutions for these dilemmas. To start with, the work of diplomats (in both models) is characterised by a great deal of discretion and autonomy. Diplomats typically operate in the international arena with relatively little direct control from hierarchical superiors (cf. Coolsaet 1998: 20). There are three reasons for this. First, the work of diplomats often requires specific expertise, which makes it difficult for others than the diplomat properly to assess the processes and outcomes that take place in the international arena. Second, hierarchical superiors often concentrate their scarce time and resources on a limited number of salient issues. Since expertise-driven international policy issues are normally not high on the domestic administrative and political agenda, hierarchical superiors may take a 'fire alarm' approach to the work of diplomats, only interfering when problems arise (cf. McCubbins and Schwartz 1984). Third, in their interaction with colleagues from other states, diplomats form networks that they can use to strengthen their position vis-à-vis their hierarchical superiors. In domestic settings, they are able to point to an 'international consensus' which they can use to reinforce claims 'at home' (cf. Haas's analysis of 'epistemic communities'; Haas 1989; 1992). Moreover, since decisions are made in international networks, the work of diplomats suffers from what scholars of public accountability have called 'the problem of the many hands', meaning that many people contribute to a single outcome and individual contributions are difficult to distinguish; it is almost impossible to find one single person responsible for any one outcome (Bovens 1998: 45-52).

In the classic diplomatic service, the tension between autonomy and control is mediated by a range of organisational instruments that are set in place to establish accountability relationships between individual diplomats and the Ministry of Foreign Affairs. Diplomats receive instructions and mandates from their Ministry of Foreign Affairs, while they are also required to report back to the Ministry on their activities, which allows the Ministry to keep tabs on what diplomats are doing abroad. Moreover, diplomatic services exhibit a strong 'esprit de corps', nurtured by the organisational characteristics discussed above, such as diplomacy as a life-long career, the practice of diplomats entering the service at the lowest levels and working their way up from there, as well as training programmes specifically designed for newly recruited diplomats. These unifying mechanisms are much more difficult to establish for the heterogeneous and dispersed set of civil servants that represent states in the new model of diplomacy. Therefore, an important question is how governments deal with the tension between the autonomy that is inherent in diplomatic work and their desire to exert a degree of control over the people who represent them abroad.

In addition to the tension between autonomy and control, both traditional and new diplomats have to deal with a range of dilemmas arising from their positions as intermediaries between the domestic bureaucracy and their international counterparts. These intermediary positions may expose diplomats to opposite claims from the 'two sides' as well as to conflicting loyalties and different senses of 'belonging'. In diplomatic services, one way to prevent diplomats from 'going native' is to establish a system of continuously changing jobs, in which diplomats typically spend only a few years at one and the same foreign post and are assigned posts at the Ministry of Foreign Affairs itself every so many years so they stay in touch with their home country. For 'non-professional' diplomats, the situation may be somewhat different, since they typically 'commute' between their home department and international forums. At the same time, this may result in new forms of 'split loyalties', as civil servants continually have to move back and forth between their national and their European roles (Thedvall 2007).

1.4 Research questions

The current literature reveals three major gaps or weaknesses that will be addressed in this book. First, there is little systematic knowledge about the (quantitative) scale of the involvement of national civil servants in EU governance. How many civil servants are involved in these kinds of activities and how important are these activities relative to 'traditional' diplomacy? What we know either rests on educated guesses based on numbers of forums or on the presence of foreign missions or officials from departments other than the Ministry of Foreign Affairs. Second, we have little insight into the daily work practices of 'new' diplomats. What do these officials *do* when they interact with colleagues from other countries? How do they deal with the tensions inherent in their positions as interlocutors between their own department and their foreign peers? Third, little is known about how national 'Eurocrats' are embedded organisationally in their home departments. How much room do they have to manoeuvre, and how are they organisationally facilitated (or constrained) in their work?

This book seeks to answers these questions by systematically studying the EU-related activities of Dutch national civil servants. More specifically, the three main questions we will answer are:

1. To what extent are Dutch civil servants involved in EU-related activities?
2. How do individual Dutch civil servants experience and practice the

craft of policy-making for and in European arenas?

3. To what extent and how are these civil servants facilitated and constrained by existing ways of organising European affairs in their respective organisations?

The first two questions relate to the *individual* dimension of a civil servant's involvement in EU affairs. They involve the following key issues:

- *role orientations*: what do national civil servants see as their chief tasks and aims when participating in European policy processes?
- *activity and contact patterns*: how much of their daily work is spent on European matters, and how do they spend that time?
- *arenas and channels*: where does 'European' policy-making 'happen' for these civil servants?
- *formal and informal 'rules of the game'*: how does policy-making unfold in these arenas?
- *effectiveness*: what do Dutch civil servants consider 'a proper job' when operating on the European stage?
- *knowledge and expertise*: what in their experience are the crucial competencies for national civil servants who operate on the European stage?

The third question pertains to the *organisational* dimension. Here we have identified the following key issues:

- *personnel policies*: how do organisations in Dutch central government recruit officials for EU-related tasks and how do these EU-related activities fit into the career development of those officials?
- *organisational structures*: how is EU-related work embedded within the organisation and how do organisations facilitate this work?
- *co-ordination processes*: how do organisations 'manage' the EU-related activities of civil servants in terms of instruction and guidance as well as co-ordination between organisational units?[2]

1.5 Methods

The questions we seek to answer are multifaceted and include both quantitative and qualitative elements. Thus, in answering them we employed a combination of research designs and data-gathering methods. This allowed us to tap into several sources of potentially relevant information and to capture a wide range of perspectives on the pertinent issues.

Population studies: Surveys

We commenced by conducting a large-scale survey among Dutch civil servants working in various departments of the national government. We had the opportunity to incorporate a number of questions on EU-related activities into a large survey on job characteristics, job satisfaction and public sector motivation administered by the Dutch Ministry of the Interior (the so-called 'POMO' survey). The survey was conducted in the first months of 2006 and was completed by 4,502 central government civil servants working (response rate of 45%). This survey allowed us to obtain a unique, quantitative assessment of the numbers and types of civil servants involved in EU decision-making, the activities they are involved in, as well as their assessments of the organisational context within which they work.

In relation to the other methods employed in this study, the survey offers an overview of overall patterns of involvement and activity among Dutch civil servants. This allows us to assess the responses to the first major question involving the extent of civil servant involvement in EU-related activities. Moreover, it allows us to obtain an overall, statistically-informed picture of the perceptions of civil servants on their activities and the organisational context within which they operate (our third question). The construction of the questionnaire and selection of respondents will be discussed in greater detail in chapter 2, along with the results of the survey.

Furthermore, the chapter on seconded national experts (SNEs) is based on a specific survey among this group of civil servants seconded to the European Commission by the Dutch government. The sample of this survey covers the entire population of current (in 2006) Dutch SNEs and more than half of all former Dutch SNEs seconded to the Commission.

Case studies: Documents, interviews, observations, and meetings of experts

In addition to the surveys, we used a number of qualitative methods to gain more insight into the actual activities and role perceptions of civil servants in their daily routines. In order to get a more in-depth view and to be able to use different methods in the same contexts, we focused the qualitative part of our study on two cases: veterinary policy and police co-operation.

These two cases were chosen because they represent a useful set of commonalities and contrasts (i.e., they have characteristics such as 'most similar' as well as 'most different' cases when considering different clusters of salient dimensions for comparison, see George and Bennett 2005). In terms of commonalities, both cases involve more than one Dutch ministry's responsibilities, which enabled us to compare two different Dutch civil service organisations operating within one and the same European domain.

At the same time, the two cases sharply contrast in terms of the timing and degree of Europeanisation of regulatory and policy activity. Veterinary policy is a longstanding EU (and international) policy field, in which participants have been meeting regularly and for prolonged periods of time, and which operates according to well-established and formalised operating procedures. Police co-operation, by contrast, is a relatively novel policy area within the EU, which is in the development stages and operates under much less fixed and formalised operating procedures. In institutional terms, the two areas differ because veterinary policy forms part of the EU's First Pillar, in which the Commission and the European Parliament play an important role, while police co-operation is part of the Third Pillar, which relies much more on co-operation between member states with a weaker role for the 'supranational' EU institutions.

Although this limited comparison can obviously not aspire to the formation of a foundation of empirical generalisations, the contrast between the two cases does enable us to shed some light on possible differences between civil service work in more and less developed governance regimes in the EU. At the European level, the issue in this context is whether Europeanised civil service practices differ across the various governance regimes (the pillars) that the EU harbours. Within the Dutch civil service, the two cases allow us to analyse whether Dutch government organisations that have been dealing with the EU for decades employ different work methods than those whose involvement is more recent.

In order to capture the variety of activities and perspectives in each of the two cases, we opted for a methodological triangulation approach that included three distinct methods. To begin with, we conducted structured, thematic interviews with 49 middle-ranking and top officials in the two policy sectors. These officials worked for four different ministries, their associated executive agencies and the Dutch Permanent Representation in the EU in Brussels. We asked them about their experiences in 'doing' European policy-making (and, to a lesser extent, policy implementation) in The Hague, in Brussels, and anywhere else their jobs took them. The interviews were recorded on tape and later transcribed. All interviewees agreed to be cited by name, but we have generally refrained from doing so unless the quotations were clearly recognisable as coming from a particular person. Likewise, interviews were conducted with 28 current and former SNEs in order to gain a more nuanced and in-depth understanding of their activities and roles.

Furthermore, we engaged in non-participant observation of the EU-related work routines of officials in different parts of the Dutch police, the Ministry of the Interior, the Ministry of Justice, the Ministry of Agriculture, Nature and Food Quality and the Food and Consumer Product Safety Authority. We attended a total of 16 meetings and/or visited relevant organisations to observe how EU-related activities take place and how the participants engage in those activities. We 'shadowed' the officials involved as they went about their jobs preparing for and participating in European meetings, mostly for one but sometimes for several full days. Shadowing amounted to a mix of non-participant observation and seizing the opportunities offered by joint travel, breaks and lunches to have more informal discussions with both the people to be shadowed and the people they interacted with. This gave us the opportunity to understand the world of Dutch Eurocrats as they themselves experienced it, at least more so than any other of the research methods used were able to. Detailed notes were kept during or immediately after the observation periods in order to document observations and impressions.

Finally, after completing all this and having drawn preliminary conclusions on the basis of the survey and the two case studies, we conducted five expert meetings with middle-ranking and top-level officials from throughout the Dutch government, to check on the broader salience of these initial findings. These meetings of experts were designed to further deepen our insights about what it means to be, and organise, national 'Eurocrats.' A total of 27 officials participated in these sessions, which lasted 2.5 hours each. Each session was taped and transcribed.

1.6 Book plan

Having outlined the theoretical and methodological background of this study, chapters 2 through 6 present the empirical results of this book. Chapter 2, which is co-authored by Ellen Mastenbroek, outlines the results of the survey of 4,502 Dutch national government civil servants. It focuses both on activities by individual civil servants and on the organisational context within which they operate. At the individual level, the chapter gives an overview of the extent and forms of EU involvement in the Dutch civil service. At the organisational level, the chapter looks at the position of EU-related activities within government organisations and the way these activities are managed and facilitated. The survey allows us to sketch an overall picture of EU activities and their organisational context that forms a useful background for the more specific, in-depth analyses of the subsequent chapters.

Chapters 3 and 4 present the results of the two case studies we conducted in the fields of veterinary policy and police co-operation, respectively. Chapter 3 focuses on veterinary policy. In their daily policy work, the actions of Europeanised civil servants are to a large extent directed towards translating their department's interests into EU policies. This chapter describes how Dutch veterinary policy Eurocrats derive and 'upload' their national preferences to the European policy process (Börzel 2002). Through extensive interviews with civil servants from the Ministry of Agriculture and subordinate agencies we were able to detect three alternative strategies that Eurocrats from this department regularly employ: frontloading, signalling and coalition formation.

Signalling consists of targeting Commission officials who are working on a given policy dossier and conveying the preferences of the national government on that dossier. Frontloading moves one step further, as member state civil servants try to become actively involved in preparing EU policy proposals. Coalition formation is used to influence debates in committees and working groups. This chapter will also show how these strategies are employed and how the decisions for one or another strategy are made.

The chapter focuses on a phase within the EU policy process that has hitherto received scant attention, but which is pivotal to any member state for which the upload of its own preferences is a strategic priority. It zooms in on one particular aspect of EU policy work: the manoeuvring that takes place during the early stages of the policy-making process in First Pillar settings, e.g., when the Commission is considering formulating a proposal. Secondly, we differ from the mainstream studies on uploading in that we focus on the strategic behaviour of individual civil servants and ministries instead of aggregated member states or European institutions (Scharpf 1997) whose parts may in fact harbour their own perceptions and pursue their own interests.

In chapter 4, we study Dutch Eurocrats in the field of European police co-operation in order to understand the worlds they work in, and the ways in which they define and do their work. We identify three quite distinct logics of Eurocratic work, i.e., different ways of operating in different European arenas. The first logic encompasses that of the bureaucrat-diplomats at the ministries as well as in working groups and committees in Brussels who bargain in the area of national positions. The second is that of street-level entrepreneurs who build transnational coalitions of the willing as they are confronted with transnational crime. The third and last logic of Eurocratic work is that of departmental co-ordinators focused on ensuring that the machinery of the domestic preparation of EU policy processes continues to function smoothly. Because these three types of civil servants work via different European action channels, the demands imposed on them and the way that their work is organisationally embedded and facilitated are very different.

Chapter 5, which is co-authored by Caspar van den Berg and Semin Suvarierol, looks at one specific type of national civil servant in the EU: seconded national experts (SNEs). The duality of national and European roles is perhaps the most profound for them since they are practically torn between two employers: their daily employer under whose supervision they work (the Commission) and the national employer who sent them on the secondment and continues to pay their salaries (the member state). Other than these atypical terms of employment, SNEs also form a particular group of European civil servants in terms of their position at a crossing point of European and national governance at the micro-level. This chapter asks if SNEs build bridges between the Commission and the member state or whether they act as national bridgeheads in the supranational Commission arena through their (transnational) networks. This chapter addresses how SNEs use their networks during and after their secondment and assesses the extent to which the SNEs and the Dutch government benefit from the secondment period in terms of exchange of information and career development.

Chapter 6 finally assembles the argument and formulates a number of conclusions based on the book's general themes.

CHAPTER 2

TOWARD A EUROPEANISED CIVIL SERVICE? A SURVEY STUDY

Co-author Ellen Mastenbroek

2.1 Surveying the Dutch civil service

Before we touch upon this book's main objective – to find out more about how Dutch national bureaucrats 'do EU business' – we first have to answer the obvious question: who are these people? How many officials in Dutch national government 'do European business' on a more than incidental basis? And which organisations within the Dutch public service do they tend to work for? Perhaps surprisingly, this obvious question has never been answered before. On the individual level, we do not know how many Dutch civil servants are involved in EU-related activities and what kinds of activities they are involved in. On the organisational level, the questions include how EU-related activities are embedded in different parts of Dutch national government and how EU-related work is managed and facilitated organisationally.

To address this deficiency, we conducted a large-scale survey among civil servants working for organisations in Dutch national government. In doing so, we were able to use data from a biennial civil servant personnel survey that the Dutch Ministry of the Interior conducts. This so-called 'POMO' survey included a range of questions concerning the jobs and careers of individual civil servants as well as their personal backgrounds. We included four questions on EU-related activities in the questionnaire for the 2006 version of the POMO survey. These questions are reproduced (translated from Dutch into English) in appendix I of this book.

In terms of population, the survey included all Dutch national government ministries, except the Ministry of Defence. Moreover, it also covered four large semi-autonomous executive agencies: Tax Department, Public Works and Water Management Agency, Immigration and Naturalisation

Services, and Prison Services. From this group of some 90,000 civil servants, a random sample of 10,000 respondents was drawn. The survey could be completed on paper or online. In the end, 4,502 civil servants responded, yielding a response rate of 45%.

The questions focused on producing an overall picture of EU involvement among civil servants as well as the organisational management of and support for EU-related job activities. To get these results, respondents were first asked to indicate if their work was affected by the EU. To emphasise the effects of the EU on their *work* (rather than their organisation, policy sector or policies in general), the question referred to a list of eight types of EU-related activities that we discerned. This list was deliberately broad, ranging from participation in Commission expert groups or Council working parties to the transposition and enforcement of EU law and activities that involve taking into account EU law and policies when working on national policies. In this way, an inclusive assessment could be made of the extent and variety of EU-related activities within the Dutch national government.

After this preliminary filter, respondents were then asked to indicate how important each of the eight types of activities were in their work, using a five-point scale from 'totally unimportant' to 'very important'. Respondents then had to indicate how many hours per week on average they spent on these EU-related activities. This allowed us to assess not only the number of civil servants working on EU-related activities but also the amount of time spent on these activities.

Finally, respondents were presented with six statements on the way their organisations managed and facilitated EU-related activities. Three of the statements were related to issues of personnel management: training opportunities, the selection of personnel for EU-related activities, and whether or not working on the EU is beneficial for one's career. The three other statements related to the policy management of EU-related work: the clarity of the mandate that civil servants receive when they go to EU meetings, the priority accorded to EU-related activities in the organisation, and the co-ordination between policymakers and implementers when it comes to EU policies. For each statement, respondents could indicate to what degree they agreed on a five-point scale, from 'I do not agree at all' to 'I totally agree'.

What follows are the results of this survey, starting with the individual level of EU involvement, and then proceeding to the organisational embeddedness and facilitation of those activities. On the basis of these results, we can draw a number of overall conclusions about Dutch national Eurocrats, which form a general background to the more specific and detailed qualitative analyses of chapters 3 and 4.

2.2 Finding Dutch 'Eurocrats'

How large does EU-related work loom in the daily existence of Dutch central government bureaucrats? How many of them can be called national 'Eurocrats' – people for whom dealing with EU matters is part of their professional core business – and for how many is the EU merely something peripheral to their jobs? The results of our survey allow us to answer these questions for a broad group of civil servants in Dutch national government. In this section, we will take a closer look at two elements of these results. First, we will outline the overall levels of EU involvement among Dutch civil servants and the amount of time they spend on EU-related work. We will then analyse the specific activities these civil servants perform and how these activities relate to each other.

Incidental versus regular participants
An important measure of EU involvement is the proportion of respondents who indicate that their work is affected by the EU. As is shown in table 2.1, approximately 30% of respondents answered in the affirmative. We will refer to this 30% of respondents as civil servants 'whose work is affected by the EU' or 'who are involved in EU-related work'. Most of the subsequent analyses are carried out solely within this group of respondents.

EU involvement	Frequency	Percent	Valid Percent
No	3066	68.1%	69.8%
Yes	1329	29.5%	30.2%
Valid total	4395	97.6%	100.0%
Missing	107	2.4%	
Total	4502	100.0%	

Table 2.1 EU involvement among civil servants (N=4502)

It is difficult to say whether 30% is a high or a low figure, because comparable data for other countries are scarce. In a survey among Norwegian civil servants, Egeberg and Trondal (1999) found that 45% of civil servants working at domestic ministries were 'affected to some extent or more' by the EU, compared to 44% at agencies and 61% at the Ministry of Foreign Affairs.[3] Likewise, an earlier study by Wessels (1997: 281) estimated that some 40% of higher (i.e., 'policy-making') German civil servants were 'directly, i.e., by their presence in Brussels, involved in one segment or other of EU policy cycles as part of their everyday duties'. In a comparative study covering four Nordic countries, Lægreid et al. (2004) reported figures ranging from 31% (Norway) to 57% (Finland and Sweden) and a high of 64% (Iceland) of respondents who thought that 'the overall consequences' of the EU on their policy area were 'fairly large' or 'very large'.

These figures are generally higher than the ones we found in our survey, but in these other surveys, either the wording of the question or the sampling method differed from our study. When it comes to wording, Lægreid et al. (2004) asked respondents whether EU policies and regulations affected their policy area, while we asked specifically about the respondents' jobs. In terms of samples, the Nordic surveys included either the EU specialists of departmental units (Lægreid et al. 2004) or only officials in positions requiring a university degree (Egeberg and Trondal 1999). Wessels's estimate, which is not based on a formal survey, also refers to higher level civil servants in the German government. This normally leads to higher figures compared to our sample, which was drawn from all employees, including support staff not directly involved in policy-related work.

We can increase the comparability of our figures with those reported by Wessels and Egeberg and Trondal by distinguishing the types of jobs and the educational levels completed by the respondents. Table 2.2 presents the figures for EU involvement broken down by job type, which respondents noted in another part of the POMO survey.

Table 2.2 shows that civil servants involved in policy preparation score highest when it comes to EU involvement at 47%, while those involved in secretarial and support jobs score below 20%. Overall, the figures for civil servants involved in policy-related jobs ('policy preparation', 'oversight', 'management' and 'policy implementation') hover around the 40% that was also noted by both Wessels and Egeberg and Trondal.

Table 2.3 presents EU involvement broken down by the level of education completed by a respondent (also a question that was included in another

Job type	Involved in EU-related work		Total number of respondents
	Percent	Frequency	Frequency
Policy preparation	47%	270	581
Oversight	43%	282	660
Management	37%	186	498
Research	35%	71	201
Policy implementation	30%	224	749
Secretariat	18%	49	275
Support	17%	144	829
Other	17%	92	558
Total	30%	1318	4351

Table 2.2 EU involvement by job type (N=4351)

part of the survey). This table shows a close association between educational level and EU involvement, with 46% of those holding university degrees
being involved in EU-related work. Again, this comes close to the figures
reported by both Wessels and Egeberg and Trondal, which suggests that the
levels of EU involvement found in the Dutch government is quite similar
to figures found in Norway and Germany in the 1990s.

Educational Level	Involved in EU-related work		Total number of respondents
	Percent	Frequency	Frequency
Primary and lower vocational education	19%	44	237
General secondary education	25%	297	1210
Intermediate and higher vocational education	26%	473	1813
University degree	46%	506	1092
Total	30%	1320	4352

Table 2.3 EU involvement by educational level (N=4352)

Being involved in EU-related work is one thing, spending time on EU-related activities is quite another. This point is illustrated by figure 2.1, which shows the average weekly number of hours spent on EU-related activities by respondents whose work was affected by the EU.

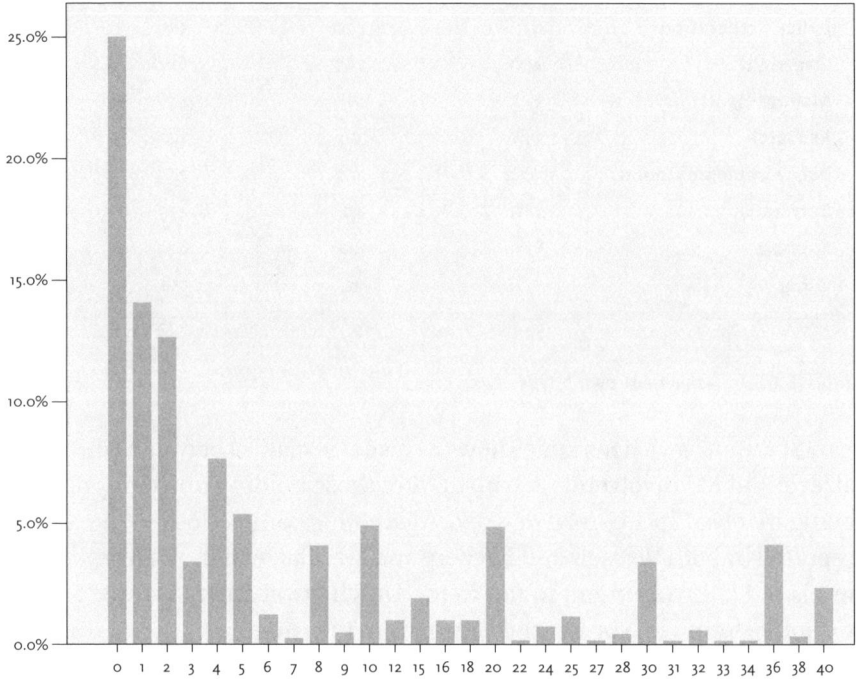

Figure 2.1 Time spent on EU-related activities by civil servants whose work is affected by the EU (N=1244)

Within the group of civil servants whose work is affected by the EU, the vast majority spends relatively little time on EU-related activities. A bit more than half of all civil servants spend two hours or less a week on EU-related activities, and almost 75% spend less than 10 hours. On the other side of the spectrum, there are peaks at 30 hours, 36 hours and 40 hours. The latter two presumably reflect a full working week for those respondents, making them the true 'Eurocrats'.[4] In terms of all the respondents (including those whose work is *not* affected by the EU), they comprise some 3% of the Dutch civil services.

The mean time spent on EU-related activities among civil servants whose work is affected by the EU is 7.81 hours per week. This figure is biased, however, by the relatively small group of respondents who report a relatively high number of hours. As a result, some 69% of civil servants in figure 2.1 spend less than the mean 7.81 hours a week on EU-related activities. An alternative and arguably less misleading way of summarising the data is therefore to look at the median time spent. For the 30% of respondents whose work is affected by the EU, the median number of hours spent on the EU is 2, which reflects the fact that an overwhelming number of these respondents spend relatively few hours on EU-related activities.

Since Dutch officials commonly work part-time, we have also looked at the time spent on EU-related work by dividing the reported number of hours by the contractual working week of each respondent. We then obtain the time spent on EU-related activities relative to the total working week. Table 2.4 shows the time shares of EU-related activities divided among four classes, ranging from less than 25% to more than 75%.

Share of contract time spent on EU	Frequency	Percentage of respondents whose work is affected by the EU
Less than 25%	918	73.9%
25-50%	113	9.1%
50-75%	76	6.1%
More than 75%	135	10.9%
Total	**1242**	**100%**

Table 2.4 Time share of EU-related work among civil servants whose work is affected by the EU (N=1242)

The majority of civil servants whose work is affected by the EU (73.9%) spend less than 25% of their contract time on the EU, while 10.9% spend more than 75% of their working week on EU-related activities. The categories between 25% and 75% together account for the remaining 15.2%. These findings indicate that EU-related activities are dispersed among a wide range of Europeanised civil servants, but that a small group spends, relatively speaking, a lot of time on the EU.

The EU participation ladder

In addition to EU involvement and the number of hours spent on EU-related activities, respondents were also asked to indicate how important eight specific EU-related activities are in their work (see question 2 in appendix 1 for the complete description of each activity). Table 2.5 shows these eight activities, ranking them in order of their importance to the work of the respondents. Respondents could choose between five different responses, ranging from 'totally unimportant' to 'very important'. In table 2.5, the 'fairly important' and 'very important' categories have been combined into an 'important' category, while the other three together form the 'unimportant' category.

EU-related activities	Important		Unimportant		Total
	Percents	Frequency	Percents	Frequency	N
Implementation	67%	852	33%	417	1269
Taking into account EU policies	51%	640	49%	619	1259
Transposition	44%	555	56%	701	1256
Bilateral consultation	33%	420	67%	843	1263
Preparation of negotiations	33%	417	67%	853	1270
Commission working groups	25%	317	75%	940	1257
Involving local government	25%	309	75%	947	1256
Council working groups	17%	211	83%	1048	1259

Table 2.5 Importance of specific EU-related activities among civil servants whose work is affected by the EU

Table 2.5 is topped by what we call 'top-down' EU-related activities, such as implementation, taking into account EU policies in domestic policy-making and the transposition of EU law into national law. These activities all relate to the impact of EU laws and policies on domestic laws and policies. 'Bottom-up' activities, which relate to the Dutch input into EU policy-making, rank much lower. Actual participation in Commission and Council working groups is important for 25% and 17% of the respondents whose work is affected by the EU, while both preparation of negotiations and bilateral consultations are important for approximately one-third of those respondents.

A relevant follow-up question regards how these activities relate to each other: do respondents specialise in one or several EU-related activities or is there considerable overlap and do civil servants tend to do most of these activities at the same time? We can answer this question by doing a principal component analysis of the eight activities. A principal component analysis is a statistical technique that allows us to uncover clusters of activities that tend to be performed together. If activities indeed belong to the same cluster, this may indicate that they represent a similar underlying type of activity.[6]

EU-related activities	Component	
	1 'Dutch input into EU policy-making'	**2** 'Implementation of EU law and policies'
Commission Working Groups	.930	
Preparation of EU meetings	.920	
Bilateral contacts	.878	
Council Working Groups	.878	
Involving local governments	.624	
Taking into account EU policies	.498	.453
Transposition	.455	.581
Enforcement		.904

Table 2.6 Factor loading of specific EU-related activities on the two extracted components (factor loading shown if they are greater than .4; the total explained variance is 73%).

Table 2.6 shows that the principal component analysis yields two such clusters (called 'components').[7] The figures in the table show how strongly each of the activities is correlated with these two components (the so-called 'factor loading' of each activity). The closer a factor loading is to 1, the stronger an activity is related to that component. Factor loadings have only been indicated if they are greater than .4.

The first component includes all specific activities except enforcement. 'Bottom-up' activities score highest on this component, while transposition scores lower on this component than on the second. As this component refers mostly to the Dutch input into EU policy-making, we labelled it accordingly. The second component consists of enforcement, transposition and taking into account EU policies when developing domestic policies, although the latter activity scores higher on the first component. These are activities that all relate to the 'top-down' activities of implementing EU law and policy.

Hence, civil servants tend to specialise to some degree in one of the two types of activity. At the same time, component 1 shows that all specific activities, with the exception of enforcement, are clustered to a considerable extent. Specialisation is therefore not absolute – there is no sharp division between the activities – but is a matter of emphasis within a wider set of activities.

A closer look at pairs of specific activities reveals that there is in fact a consistent pattern in the relations between them. Table 2.7 illustrates this well; it shows the relationship between participation in both Council and Commission working groups.[8] The columns show the percentages of respondents who find participation in Commission Working Groups unimportant and important, respectively. The rows indicate how many respondents find

			Participation in Commission Working Groups		Total
			Unimportant	Important	
Participation in Council Working Groups	Unimportant	% within Council Working Groups	87.0%	13.0%	1039
		% within Commission Working Groups	96.7%	43.7%	
	Important	% within Council Working Groups	14.8%	85.2%	210
		% within Commission Working Groups	3.3%	57.0%	
Total		Count	935	314	1249

Table 2.7 Cross table between 'Importance of participation in Council Working Groups' and 'Importance of participation in Commission Working Groups', based on the dichotomous variables for each (N=1249)

participation in Council Working Groups (un)important. The percentages of '% within Council Working Groups' add up to 100% across rows, while the percentages of % within Commission Working Groups' add up across columns.

The percentages in the table reveal that the association between the two activities is not symmetrical. The vast majority of those who find participation in Council groups important also find participation in Commission groups important (85%). However, a much smaller proportion of those who find participation in Commission groups important also find participation in Council groups important (57%).

As noted in table 2.5, participation in Council working groups is important for only 17% of all respondents, compared to 25% for whom participation in Commission working groups is important. The group of respondents for whom participation in Council working groups is important therefore forms a subset of the larger group of respondents for whom participation in Commission working groups is important.

This pattern also holds for other pairs of specific activities, such as the preparation of EU meetings and participation in Council and Commission groups, or transposition and enforcement. It also holds for pairs of activities that belong to different components in table 2.6: 78% of respondents for whom participation in Council working groups is important also find enforcement important, but vice versa, only 20% of those for whom enforcement is important also find participation in Council working groups important.

Therefore, table 2.5 presents a sort of overall 'participation ladder' of EU-related activities. Civil servants who are engaged in more specialised activities (such as participation in Council working groups) are also engaged in more widespread activities (up to and including enforcement), but not the other way around.

2.3 The organisational context of Dutch Eurocracy

Individual involvement and activities only tell part of the story of Dutch 'Eurocracy'. Individual civil servants operate within an organisational context that facilitates some and constrains other activities. In this section, we will shed more light on this organisational context and the implications it has for the work of individual civil servants.

Organisational pockets or organisational cores?

The figures regarding the number of civil servants whose work is affected by the EU (30%) and the average time they spend on EU-related activities are not likely to be the same for all parts of the Dutch national government. Instead, we expect that some organisations will show much higher levels of EU involvement than others. Moreover, apart from overall EU involvement in an organisation, it is also important to look at the way EU-related work is embedded within it. Is EU-related work the province of a small number of specialists or is it spread across a wide range of civil servants? To assess this, we constructed a 'dispersion index', which measures the extent to which the time spent on EU-related activities is distributed evenly across all of the respondents whose work is affected by the EU.[9] A value close to 0 indicates that some people spend a lot of time on EU-related activities while others spend little or no time on them. A value of 1, by contrast, indicates that all civil servants spend the same amount of time on EU-related activities.

This measure is not dependent on the level of EU involvement in an organisation. For example, if two people in an organisation are involved in EU-related work and they each spend one hour per week on the EU, the dispersion index will be 1. If, by contrast, five people spend 10 hours a week and five others 30 hours, the index will be 0.8. Even if overall EU involvement is higher in the latter organisation, the level of dispersion is lower because the time spent on EU-related work is spread more unevenly.[10]

Table 2.8 shows, for all organisations included in our survey, the percentage of respondents which indicated that their work was affected by the EU, the median time spent on EU-related activities by those respondents, and the dispersion index among them.

Based on these figures, we can discern three types of organisation. The first type, which we call 'Eurocratic bulwarks', consists of four organisations where more than 50% of all civil servants are involved in EU-related work: the Ministries of Agriculture; Foreign Affairs; Transport, Public Works and Water Management; and Economic Affairs. The median time spent on EU-related activities by respondents in these organisations is also above the overall median of 2.0 hours (up to 8.0 hours in the Ministry of Agriculture). In terms of dispersion, the differences are less pronounced, although all four ministries score above the overall dispersion index score of 0.31. Again, the Ministry of Agriculture has by far the highest score, indicating that the time spent on EU-related activities is relatively evenly spread among civil servants who work on EU-related matters.

Organisation	Involved in EU-related work	Median time spent on EU-related activities (among civil servants affected by the EU)	Dispersion index (among civil servants affected by the EU)	Number of respondents
Ministry of Agriculture	61%	8.0	0.47	276
Ministry of Foreign Affairs	56%	4.0	0.32	113
Ministry of Transport and Water Management	52%	3.0	0.35	111
Ministry of Economic Affairs	52%	4.0	0.34	115
Ministry of Social Affairs	38%	1.5	0.27	114
Ministry of Housing and the Environment	37%	2.0	0.31	167
Ministry of Finance	37%	4.0	0.33	100
Immigration Service	34%	2.0	0.22	101
Ministry of Health	33%	2.0	0.35	141
Tax Department	31%	4.0	0.34	1237
Public Works and Water Management Directorate	31%	2.0	0.32	340
Ministry of the Interior	30%	2.0	0.25	86
'Hoog College van Staat'	25%	1.0	(0.49)	52
Ministry of Education	18%	2.0	0.38	116
Ministry of Justice	17%	1.0	0.16	687
Ministry of General Affairs	17%	1.0	(1.00)	12
Prison Services	11%	0.0	0.10	554
Other	39%	2.0	0.28	66
Total	30%	2.0	0.31	4388

Table 2.8 EU involvement, median time spent and dispersion index by government organisation (N=4388)

The second type may be called the 'Eurocratic runners-up'. It consists of organisations where between 30 and 40% of civil servants are involved in EU-related work. The median number of hours spent on EU-related activities is 2.0 for most organisations in this group, but lower for the Ministry of Social Affairs (1.5 hours) and higher for the Ministry of Finance and the Tax

Service (4.0 hours).The dispersion index for organisations in this group hovers around 0.30, which is the overall score across all civil servants in our sample, with a low of 0.25 (Ministry of the Interior) and a high of 0.35 (Ministry of Health).

Finally, the third group consists of organisations that are much less involved with the EU and that we can therefore call 'national champions'. In each of these organisations, less than 30% of civil servants are involved in any EU-related work, and the median number of hours spent on EU-related activities is typically below the overall median of 2.0 hours. For the Ministry of Justice and Prison Services, the dispersion index is also much lower, indicating that most EU-related activities are carried out by a small number of EU-specialists. For other organisations, however, the picture is less clear. For instance, only 18% of respondents in the Department of Education indicate that they are involved in EU-related work, but among them, the time spent on EU-related activities is spread out relatively evenly.

The differences between organisations found in this study correspond with those found by Egeberg and Trondal (1999) in Norway. The ministries most affected by the EU in their study were Foreign Affairs, Economic Affairs and Transport, which conform to three of our four 'Eurocratic bulwarks'. The Ministry of Agriculture is missing from the Norwegian list, but this is presumably because Norway is not a member of the EU and therefore does not participate in the EU's Common Agricultural Policy.

Our findings do differ, however, from those of Laffan and O'Mahoney (2007) in Ireland. They also argue that Ireland's central government consists of three circles of EU involvement, but identify different ministries. Their 'Holy Trinity' of most strongly Europeanised ministries are Foreign Affairs, Finance and the Prime Minister's Office. The Ministry of Foreign Affairs is the only one of these three that also appears among our European top four. Laffan and O'Mahoney's second circle consists of an 'inner core' of ministries dealing with key EU areas, such as agriculture, justice, industry, trade and employment, and the environment. Some of these ministries (Agriculture, and Economic Affairs for both enterprises and trade) are in our top category (with the Ministry of Agriculture almost forming a league of its own), while justice-related organisations (the Ministry of Justice as well as Immigration and Naturalisation Service and the Prison Services) score relatively low in our study.[15] Laffan and O'Mahoney's 'outer core' consists of ministries that have very little to do with the EU and includes, among others, the Ministry of Transportation, one of the 'top players' in both our and the Norwegian surveys.

These striking differences between Laffan and O'Mahoney and our study are probably largely the result of different methods used to establish categorisations. Whereas our study relies on a survey among civil servants in governmental organisations, Laffan and O'Mahoney make a qualitative assessment of the relative prominence of certain government ministries in EU affairs. Although prominence is an important issue in policy-making, it arguably offers a less firm basis for assessing the overall impact of the EU on governmental organisations. This, we argue, is better assessed by looking at actual activities.

Coming back to our own results, it is striking that the three indicators for the degree of Europeanisation of organisations tend to go together: not only do Eurocratic bulwarks have higher numbers of civil servants doing EU-related work, but these civil servants also tend to devote more time to EU-related activities and the time spent on these activities tends to be spread more evenly across the civil servant population. With some exceptions, the opposite is true for the 'national champions' in our sample. The middle category of 'Eurocratic runners-up' tends to fall inbetween on all three indicators, however, with notable exceptions for some organisations when it comes to the median number of hours spent and the level of dispersion.

Of course, the lines between the three categories are somewhat arbitrary, in particular when it comes to differentiating between the 'Eurocratic runners-up' and the 'national champions'. What the figures do show, however, is that there are substantial differences between organisations in terms of how Europeanised they are and also the extent to which EU-related activities have become part of the organisational 'core'. This three-fold distinction therefore offers a good starting point for the further analysis of the organisational dynamics around EU-related work in Dutch national government, an issue we will turn to next.

Embedded Eurocratic work: Organisational support vs neglect

As we have seen above, organisations in one Dutch central government differ in how central EU-related activities are to the work of their civil servants. We can expect that these differences will affect the way that EU matters are managed and facilitated organisationally. In order to test this expectation, we have analysed the responses to the six statements on this issue in our survey.

Table 2.9 shows the overall responses. The keywords refer to the six statements, the exact wording of which can be found in question 4 of appendix 1.

Three of the statements related to personnel management (training opportunities, selection criteria for EU-related jobs, and career prospects for people working on the EU), while the other three covered issues of policy management (the clarity of mandates for EU meetings, the priority given to
EU-related work, and the co-ordination between policymakers and policy
implementers).

Statement	Completely disagree	Largely disagree	Neither agree nor disagree	Largely agree	Completely agree	N
Training	8%	18%	27%	35%	12%	810
Selection	9%	16%	43%	28%	4%	661
Career	15%	15%	32%	28%	10%	772
Mandate	11%	14%	44%	22%	9%	504
Priority	20%	32%	28%	14%	6%	802
Co-ordination	9%	19%	37%	27%	8%	668

Table 2.9 Overall responses to the six statements

These overall results show a mildly positive response to all of the statements, bearing in mind that the statement on priority was formulated in a
negative way so that 'disagree' becomes a positive response. How, then, do
responses vary among survey participants?

On the individual level, we can look at the correlation between the responses to the six statements and the amount of time respondents spend on
EU-related activities. As it turns out, all of these correlations are negative,
ranging from -.3 to -.4, and are thus highly significant.[16] Hence, the more respondents are involved in EU-related work, the less positive they are about
both personnel and policy management in their organisation. The only exception is the statement on priority because the more time respondents
spend on EU-related activities, the more positive they are about the priority
given to EU-related work. Still, overall, personnel and policy management
were judged most positively by respondents for whom EU-related work is
only a small part of their job.

This does not imply that organisations with relatively high levels of EU
involvement are also judged more negatively by their employees. Quite the
contrary, table 2.10 shows that respondents are generally more positive the
more 'Europeanised' their organisations are. In table 2.10, we distinguish

between the three types of organisation that we discussed above. For each statement, the 'do not agree' and 'do not agree at all' categories have been combined under the category 'disagree', while the original answers 'agree' and 'totally agree' are combined under the 'agree' category.

Statement	Type of organisation	Disagree	Neutral	Agree	N
Training	National champions	37%	21%	42%	83
	Eurocratic runners-up	25%	28%	47%	465
	Eurocratic bulwarks	24%	28%	48%	260
Selection	National champions	33%	31%	36%	64
	Eurocratic runners-up	25%	47%	28%	374
	Eurocratic bulwarks	24%	39%	38%	221
Career	National champions	38%	23%	38%	73
	Eurocratic runners-up	33%	35%	32%	449
	Eurocratic bulwarks	25%	29%	46%	248
Mandate	National champions	26%	38%	36%	47
	Eurocratic runners-up	27%	50%	23%	279
	Eurocratic bulwarks	22%	36%	42%	176
Priority	National champions	39%	34%	27%	82
	Eurocratic runners-up	49%	30%	21%	454
	Eurocratic bulwarks	62%	24%	14%	264
Co-ordination	National champions	31%	36%	34%	59
	Eurocratic runners-up	28%	42%	30%	386
	Eurocratic bulwarks	28%	37%	43%	221

Table 2.10 *Responses to the six statements by respondents in the three types of organisations*

The statement on training does not reveal any major differences, although respondents from national champions tend to agree a bit less often than respondents in Eurocratic runners-up and Eurocratic bulwarks. For the other five statements, respondents in Eurocratic bulwarks are consistently more positive than respondents in the other two types of organisation, again bearing in mind that 'disagree' is a positive answer when it comes to the statement on the priority given to EU-related work. The 'negative' responses ('disagree' for most statements, and 'agree' for the statement on priority), show the same pattern, but with smaller differences.

Although Eurocratic bulwarks score consistently higher than the other types of organisation, this is not true for Eurocratic runners-up vis-à-vis national champions. In fact, for the statements on selection, career prospects, mandates and co-ordination, national champions score higher levels of positive responses than the Eurocratic runners-up.[17] Meanwhile, in the negative response categories, by contrast, the differences are more consistent, with Eurocratic runners-up scoring higher than national champions.

These results suggest that the core division between organisations in the Dutch central government is between highly Europeanised Eurocratic bulwarks and the rest. In Eurocratic bulwarks, two of the statements on personnel management (those relating to selection and career prospects, respectively) were responded to more positively, as were all of the statements regarding policy management. The fact that respondents who spend more time on the EU tend to be more critical may reflect the fact that the management of EU-related work is more important to them than it is to people who are only tangentially involved in EU-related activities. This tendency at the individual level notwithstanding, the analysis shows that respondents become more positive when their organisation reaches a certain threshold of Europeanisation. This is another indication that EU-related work in those organisations has moved from the periphery to the core of what the organisation is doing.

2.4 The virtuous spiral of organisational Europeanisation

The data from our survey support two major conclusions. In terms of individual involvement in EU-related work, some 30% of respondents indicate that their work is affected by the EU. Within this category, however, the vast majority of civil servants spend relatively little time on EU-related activities. As a result, EU-related work seems to remain somewhat of a specialised activity in the Dutch national government. Besides a relatively broad group of civil servants for whom the EU is only of peripheral concern, there is a smaller group of civil servants who spend all or most of their time on the EU. The group inbetween is relatively small by comparison. In that sense, EU-related work remains the domain of pockets of specialists within the Dutch national government.

At the same time, these overall figures obscure important variations on the organisational level. In some organisations, more than half of all civil servants are involved in EU-related work, whereas in other organisations this figure is 20% or less. Furthermore, higher levels of EU involvement tend to correlate with both higher median numbers of hours spent on EU-related activities and a wider dispersion of EU-related work among civil servants. Therefore, EU-related work on all counts tends to be much closer to the core of what organisations are doing when the work of more people in these organisations is affected by the EU.

These differences are also reflected in the way organisations manage and facilitate EU-related work. Respondents in organisations with high levels of EU involvement are more positive about the way EU-related activities are integrated in personnel management as well as the way EU policy processes are managed.

Overall, then, our findings suggest that there is a *'virtuous spiral of Europeanisation'* in Dutch central government organisations: the more civil servants are involved in EU-related work, the better it is managed and facilitated. This, one may assume, will in turn lead to a greater awareness of EU-related activities within the organisation and hence greater EU involvement. The findings also suggest that there may be a *critical threshold* for this effect to occur. Our data show small differences between moderately and weakly Europeanised organisations, but a strong difference between highly Europeanised organisations (which we called 'Eurocratic bulwarks') and the rest. In our survey, the threshold lies at approximately 50% of civil servants being involved in EU-related work. This specific figure may be a result of characteristics of the Dutch national government or of the organisations that were included in our survey. In general, however, this type of threshold effect may well be present in other EU-member states and other parts of government as well.

CHAPTER 3

EUROCRATIC WORK AS STRATEGIC BEHAVIOUR: MOVING BEFORE THE COMMISSION DOES IN VETERINARY POLICY

3.1 Representing the 'national interest' in Brussels

The senior echelons of the various departments that national Eurocrats work for expect them to make sure their department's view of the world is successfully presented when EU policies are being created (or implemented). To do this job well, Eurocrats need to know about the plans and intentions of 'their' Directorate-General at the European Commission early on in the policy process. Furthermore, they need to be able to sense where the Commission is heading with a particular proposal; assess the implications for their department in terms of costs and benefits for the domestic policy status quo; discuss these plans with their colleagues in other units within their own department or with colleagues with related or affected portfolios in other departments; involve external experts and write reports; and finally, determine their department's position with regard to the specific policy issue at hand. Their socialisation on the job and their work routines are geared towards performing these tasks.

The literature on Europeanisation abounds with 'big picture' studies of the politics of the European public policy-making process (Wessels and Rometsch 1996; Scharpf 2001; Green-Cowles et al 2001; Featherstone and Radaelli 2003), but there is surprisingly little research on the behaviour of the countless individual officials that lie at the core of the process (Thedvall 2006; Larue 2006). This chapter takes the latter view. It examines how individual Dutch civil servants *practice* public policy-making for and within European arenas. By employing this focus, we aim to shed a different light on the question of where 'European' policy-making 'happens' and how – in our case, Dutch – civil servants 'make it happen'.

We will, however, look beyond just the practices of individual Eurocrats.

The strategic interaction with other Eurocrats is part and parcel of a civil servant's work, which includes colleagues from other member countries, their superiors at their home departments, and the officials of the Commission and the Secretariat of the Council. Getting things done in Europe entails a strategic effort to produce timely, coherent and sensible national policy positions, and to build support for these at the European level. Thus, the work of most individual Eurocrats is embedded in two arenas of strategic interaction: departmental and interdepartmental preparation and the co-ordination arenas at the national level; and Commission and Council Secretariat counterparts and arenas at the European level. Hence we examine the work of departmental Eurocrats in terms of strategic manoeuvring within and between those arenas. We look at how they are instructed and guided by their superiors, how they give and receive feedback and how they are held accountable for and render account for their actions.

We are not concerned with covering the role and various behaviour patterns of Eurocrats during the full policy cycle. Our focus is limited to a specific phase therein, i.e., the pre-proposal phase, which we will elaborate upon below. This chapter is therefore situated within the broader category of 'uploading' studies (Börzel 2002), e.g., the process of advocating departmental preferences, transforming these into national positions, and introducing these at the various EU levels during the policy development phase. Obviously, policy development in the real world does not stop at this particular stage, and the politics of policy formulation continues into the implementation phase. Once a policy package has arrived at the comitology stage, the representatives of member states within the management boards of the committees will continue to bend and shape the process and output of the policies agreed upon to fit these into their national preferences (Brandsma 2006).

3.2 Uploading in the pre-proposal phase

Uploading is defined here as the actions undertaken on behalf of member states to ensure that as much of the legislative output of the EU as possible produces policies that are in line with pre-existing national policies and/or national policy preferences. Uploading can be considered a process of competition between member states (Héritier et al. 1996; Eising and Kohler-Koch 1999). Successful uploads of national preferences will reduce adaptation costs when adopted policies are 'downloaded' once they have been enacted at the European level. It will further reduce costs of transposition in pure legislative-administrative terms as well as the political transaction costs that accompany legislative bargaining (Steunenberg 2006; Mastenbroek 2007). Successful uploading will also reduce uncertainty and the costs of adaptation for the affected industry at home (Haverland 2000). Finally, as Börzel points out, successful uploading can relieve the domestic political elites of the social problems they are unable to tackle at the domestic level, such as immigration and organised crime (Börzel 2002).

Uploading studies come in various guises. We distinguish between two different streams.[18] One entails game-theoretic studies which depict European bargaining as connected or nested games. The hallmark of these games is that the same actors are involved in a whole network of games, with the outcome of one game having consequences for the start of another game. Thus actors play multiple games simultaneously or sequentially. They are thus continuously contemplating not only the strategies of the other actors involved and the outcomes of current games but also the actor strategies and outcomes of games that follow or occur at the same time as the current game (Tsebelis 1990; Putnam 1988; Mayer 1992). Relationships between the EU and member states have often been modelled as two- or even three-level (subnational, national and European) games (Pahre 1997; Payne 2000). A second strand of uploading literature includes studies of the national and supranational co-ordination of EU policies which focus, respectively, on the co-ordination of member states' national positions at home through what Schneider and Baltz (2005) have dubbed as 'Byzantine co-ordination structures', and on how member states' formal representatives at Brussels lobby for the adoption of these national positions in Brussels. In these works, member state adaptation to and shaping of European policies are being studied chiefly through the lens of formal co-ordination arrangements, e.g. interdepartmental working groups, Permanent Representative offices and the manifold EU-level groups and committees (Harmsen 1999; Kassim et al. 2000; Kassim et al. 2001; Peters and Wright 2000).

This part of our study differs from these predecessors in two important respects. The first is that we focus on the pre-proposal phase. This phase has hitherto received scant attention in EU studies, but offers crucial opportunities to any self-interested member state seeking to upload its preferences. The pre-proposal phase entails the manoeuvring that takes place during the early stages of the policy-making process in First Pillar settings, when the Commission is considering formulating a proposal. At this stage of the policy process, the Commission has the exclusive right to set the agenda, launch new policy ideas, and draft and submit proposals to the Council and European Parliament. National governments have 'strong incentives... to monitor the Commission services so that when the early signs of action are detected the interested departments at home can be alerted and begin to take steps to decide a policy' (Kassim 2001: 16). Remarkably, however, there is scant attention within the academic literature to the strategies member state governments employ during the proposal formation (or pre-proposal) stage. The majority of studies on the European policy process focus on the formal structures of national position co-ordination *after* the Commission has launched its position (Kassim et al. 2001, 2003) or deal exclusively with the decision-making process at the supranational level (Eberlein and Kerwer 2004; Thomson et al. 2006).

Secondly, our study of pre-proposal phase uploading is unique in that we focus on the strategic behaviour of individual civil servants and ministries. Existing studies focus on member states or European institutions as aggregate actors, examining their strategies. Although, for example, Börzel (2002) acknowledges that the uploading strategies (which she labelled as 'pace-setting', 'foot-dragging', and 'fence-sitting') may vary from policy sector to policy sector, her model addresses the strategy choices of member states at an aggregate level. One notable exception is the work of Schneider and Baltz (2005). They examine the discretionary powers of national governments in the preparatory stage of European legislation, but their focus rests exclusively on the strategic interactions between ministries and domestic interest groups in the formulation of the national position.

Whilst useful in its own right, the aggregate approach only goes so far (cf. Scharpf 1997). Given the high degree of sectoralisation of European policy-making it is rather a bold assumption to treat member states as unitary actors. Clearly, each of these aggregate actors is composed of other actors which have a certain capacity to act autonomously based on their own interests and perceptions. A series of Scandinavia-based studies has addressed individual civil servants, but the focus of these studies has been on the roles of individual officials' role orientations and conceptions within Europeanised arenas, such as the committees and working groups of the European Commission and the Council of Ministers, and not on their actual roles in uploading and other strategic interactions in the EU policy process (Beyers 2005; Beyers and Trondal 2004; Egeberg 1999; Trondal 2002; Trondal and Veggeland 2003). In fact, by all accounts, the EU-lobbying behaviour of national civil servants is relatively understudied when compared to private interest groups (Mazey and Richardson 1993; Van Schendelen

1998, 2006; Coen 1998; Woll 2006). The remainder of this chapter therefore explores the types of strategic instruments national ministries employ and individual civil servants apply when they 'upload.'

Uploading is a strategy aimed at ensuring that a member state's status quo within a given policy area is left untouched as much as possible. When successful, it can be highly beneficial to member states, at least from an opportunity-costs perspective. It can be 'an effective strategy to maximise the benefits and to minimise the costs of European policies' because 'the more a European policy fits the domestic context, the lower the adaptation costs in the implementation process' (Börzel 2002: 196). What is at stake are the member states' existing or preferred 'modes of governance.' For example, the Dutch approach to hygiene inspections in slaughterhouses, which is self-regulation by the business sector, contrasts sharply with the more public and state-directed approaches such as in Italy. Which country should adapt to the other country's national system? Who will bear the costs?

Making EU policy on any given subject forges a confluence of hitherto divergent national 'modes of governance.' Eising and Kohler-Koch (1999: 271) have noted that:

> EC decision making does not start in a vacuum, but in a setting of varying national modes of governance. And precisely because the EC is still in its formative phase, the actors are struggling to introduce what they consider to be the most appropriate mode of governance ... The negotiation of Community policies is always a competition about modes of governance.

In this setting, member states are in (latent) competition regarding the best models of integration. The conflicts are partly ideological, in some areas, pitting liberals against pro-interventionists. But they may also derive something from the different potential consequences of (negative or positive co-ordination) policies for the various member states, and in particular, specific policy sectors and interest groups within them (Hix 2002: 215).

Given these stakes, all stakeholders face the tactical question of when and where to upload. The ideal timing of uploading policy preferences, according to Kassim, is 'before the Commission has considered it [an issue] or before it has drafted a text' (Kassim 2001: 16). In formal EU legislative process terms, this is the stage just before the Commission releases a green or white paper on a topic and instigates consultations for new legislation or initiates a legislative process. Once the Commission has adopted a proposal, it enters the EU legislative process and will be dealt with under one of three legislative procedures (i.e., consultation, co-decision or co-operation).

The position of the Commission in the legislative process is crucial. 'Nothing', as Peterson writes (2002: 88), 'can become Community legislation unless the college [of commissioners] chooses to propose it.'[19] The importance of this prerogative cannot be underestimated.[20] During the process of proposal formation, the Commission has a variety of discretionary powers to shape the content of the final proposal (Larsson 2003). For example, the Commission enjoys the power to initiate and control expert committees. The Commission herewith not only learns the positions of member states by inviting their experts to appear before these committees, but also benefit from the expertise to improve the quality of their proposal. Or as Wessels and Rometsch (1996: 226) argue:

> the Commission controls the game in this phase and its basic strategy is one of *'engrenage'* ... i.e., to include relevant national civil servants and representatives of lobby groups early enough in its work to get additional information and insights ... From the point of view of the national civil servants, there is an expectation that their input will be taken seriously by the Commission and that its later proposals will not include unpleasant surprises for them.

Even when mutuality forms the underlying culture of the relationship between the Commission and the national civil servants, the relationship is in fact unequal, to the advantage of the Commission. First, the Commission may, for example:

> set up an expert group to find out whether the Member States and interest groups are interested in trying to formulate a common position. But should the Commission discover ... that the support for a common approach is rather weak or seems to go in an unwanted direction, it can hold the group on hold, waiting for the right moment to reactivate it (Larsson 2003: 18).

Other powerful instruments are the selection of the chairman and the selection and appointment of the participants. As Larsson (2003: 18) observes: 'allowing just a few experts, interest groups or Member States' representatives to be part of a group ... is a strategic decision that may affect the result and functioning of an expert group profoundly.'

There are clearly potentially significant 'first mover' advantages for member states if they manage to influence the contents of the Commission's proposal before it is sent into the formal legislative process. To examine whether this is in fact the case, and which types and combinations of uploading strategies work to bring this about, requires a systematic analysis of the so-called pre-proposal or policy development phase as an arena in which member states display strategic behaviour in order to influence the position of the Commission (Larsson 2003). Our focus here is only a building block towards this more general aim. We examine the strategic behaviour of individual civil servants and their ministries during the pre-proposal stage.

3.3 Research design

Data was collected from interviews with twenty-three Dutch civil servants working within the field of veterinary policy, especially on issues concerning animal welfare, animal diseases and consumer safety. Semi-structured interviews were conducted between November 2005 and July 2006 with sixteen civil servants from the Ministry of Agriculture, Nature and Food Safety (hereafter referred to as Agriculture), one from the Ministry of Public Health, Welfare and Sports (hereafter referred to as Public Health),[21] three from the Food and Consumer Product Safety Authority (*Voedsel en Warenautoriteit*; hereafter referred to as VWA), one at the Institute of Food Safety (IFS), and two respondents from the Dutch Permanent Representation to the EU. This group of respondents includes higher civil servants as well as middle-level civil servants from both ministries and agencies. The sample also covers a variety of backgrounds: scientific veterinary experts, policy coordinators and director and generalist departmental managers.

The fact that the observations in this chapter cover only a single policy area clearly limits this study. Still, at this exploratory stage of this kind of uploading research, this policy (sub)area constitutes a relevant empirical domain. It is both a well-established and crucial EU policy area. The health and welfare of farm animals is a precondition for bilateral or multilateral trade. The institutionalisation of animal health and welfare regulation predates the establishment of the EEC and became an integral part of the EU's agricultural policies.[22] In recent years, issues regarding the regulation of animal disease and welfare have been at the centre of international trade conflicts (e.g., export bans on unhealthy animals) and the subject of disputes between consumer organisations and/or animal rights organisations and the government. Finally, this policy area is rife with debate between member states because the regulation of animal disease and welfare is also part of a fundamental debate between member states on regulatory styles or modes of governance (cf. Knill 2001). The Netherlands, for example, prefers the deregulation of meat hygiene inspections, whereby the state delegates the treatment of animals and the hygiene at slaughterhouses to private firm; whereas Italy maintains direct public supervision of the slaughterhouses by departmental inspectors.

It is difficult to say at this stage if veterinary policy is a typical or an atypical, even 'crucial' (George and Bennett 2005) case when it comes to the study of uploading. However, being a fully Europeanised and institutionalised area, the strategic behaviour at the pre-proposal phase may at least reveal the shape of things to come in other Europeanising policy areas. The insights gained from this research may indicate the 'natural' evolution of strategic behaviour of other national ministries the more their policy areas are integrated into the EU. In other words, as more governments and departments are confronted with the (forced) implementation of EU policies that are less preferred, the more we can expect goal-seeking strategic interactions at this initial phase of the policy process.

3.4 Frontloading, signalling and coalition formation in veterinary policy

From our interview data we were able to induce three recurrently mentioned forms of strategic behaviour that Dutch civil servants have employed to upload their department's preferred policy preferences in an early as possible phase of preparatory policy-making by the Commission. We refer to three types of strategic behaviour: 'signalling', 'frontloading', and 'coalition formation'.[23]

Signalling the Commission entails targeting and informing specific Commission officials who work on policy issues that are important to the member state and/or the national ministerial department. Lobbying designated Commission services by civil servants working as permanent representatives, is an example of this strategy. They inform Commission officials about their department's position. The latter may use the information as an input to the proposal, provided that the member state's information is valuable to the Commission.

Frontloading goes one step further than signalling. It consists of acts designed to have a direct and substantive influence on the writing of a Commission proposal. The appointment of seconded national experts (SNEs, see also chapter 5) within the relevant Commission Directorate-General is the central strategic instrument for frontloading. An SNE is either instructed by his superiors to steer the proposal towards the department's ideal point, or it is expected that the SNE will 'automatically' choose his or her national-cultural perspective as a point of reference when writing the proposal.

Once the Commission has initiated a proposal, a member state can seek to *form coalitions* with other member states if the position of the Commission is further away from a member state's position. This strategy will typically unfold during committee meetings with national experts and civil servants (Larsson 2003; Rhinard, 2002). However, we expect this strategy to be the least preferred of the three. It is more cumbersome and 'diluted' than the other two, as it requires the forging of a critical mass of member states with preferences not too divergent (and all the compromises and horse-trading this entails). Moreover, the Commission is well-positioned to dominate the committee, as it decides who sits on it, chairs it, and so on (Larsson 2003: 73). In the remainder of this section we will describe how Dutch civil servants employ the three strategies, assess the conditions of their effectiveness, and reflect on the risks associated with them.

Signalling the Commission

Signalling implies a sender choosing to send a message to a receiver, in the hope that the receiver will then choose to act upon the message received. In EU policy, national Eurocrats send messages to the relevant Commission officials with the purpose of persuading them to choose an action that will benefit the former. This is the basic principle underlying all lobbies. In the practice of EU policy processes, civil servants engage in as much lobbying as private interest groups. Signalling could in fact be described as the lobbying of the Commission, not by private interests but by the member states themselves.

Research on the member state lobbying of the Commission is sparse, however. The best account is from Kassim et al.'s volume on the role of Permanent Representations (2001). Located at the heart of the Union, permanent representatives fulfil many tasks for the various departments within their respective member states, such as foreseeing opportunities, collecting and circulating information, and elaborating negotiation strategies (Kassim 2001: 11). The role of civil servants at the Permanent Representation is crucial, especially at the pre-proposal phase if they:

propose action before the Commission has considered it or before it has drafted a text ... This requires the assiduous cultivation of contacts by national officials in the Permanent Representation and domestic ministries with their opposite numbers in the Commission (Kassim 2001: 16):

According to one of our respondents, signalling is an increasingly salient component of the job descriptions and work routines of Eurocrats working at the Permanent Representation. Signalling forms their core business. They know Brussels and their task is to inform and be kept informed on all matters that are relevant to their field of expertise and are of interest to their department. Civil servants at the Permanent Representation are expected to successfully place:

> ... issues on the agenda of the Commission that are of importance to the Netherlands. In this way, we help the Commission with experience we have as a member state and you immediately learn it when the Commission does not think much of the information (*Permanent Representation official*).

Signalling is more than just agenda-setting and involves 'talking to the people in the Commission who are going to write the proposal' (*Ministry of Agriculture official*) and thus to direct the text of the final proposal closer to the preferences of the department. However, signalling is not a one-way process, but based on reciprocity. Information is a very precious asset to both sides:

> The Commission always wants to be kept informed. That is an issue that is often forgotten in The Hague. When something happens in a member state [e.g., the outbreak of an animal disease], other member states contact the Commission. The Commission always wants to provide answers to those member states. If the Commission fails to do so, danger exists that member states will take action by themselves, something that is not desired, of course. This way unity will be lost. I always try to prevent this by having contact [with the Commission] as much as I can so that I can contact them each time something occurs. So I can keep the Commission updated (*Permanent Representation official*).

Signalling as described above is not only part of the job of Permanent Representation officials, but increasingly that of civil servants in The Hague
as well. This signalling can take various forms, from 'just giving a call' to
asking for a draft of an upcoming report or 'stepping into a Commission official's office' when a national civil servant happens to be in Brussels for a
meeting (*VWA official*). The nationality of the Commission officials is an important issue here. Although our respondents told us that nationality played
no major role in the approaching of a Commission official, it was clear from
their further explications that the presence of Dutch people within the Commission services (both permanent as well as seconded national civil servants; see more below) can make a difference. Dutch Commission officials
more often than not contact their national departments when they receive
information on specific subjects. They are also more easily approachable by
their compatriots, notwithstanding the fact that Dutch commission officials
consider themselves to be acting in strict accordance with Commission
guidelines concerning loyalty and neutrality.

Most interviewees regard signalling to be the most effective when it is
embedded in enduring relationships between national Eurocrats and Commission officials. They claimed that trust is the most important aspect in
building and maintaining lasting and effective relationships between national and Commission officials:

> I work a lot on personal relationships. I know two Commission direc-
> tors very well. When I arrive, they know something is happening.
> Whenever there are conflicts I've always been keen on seeing the prob-
> lems from their perspective as well and not just trying to get the most
> out of it for the Netherlands (*Ministry of Agriculture official*).

The same interviewee, a very senior civil servant within the department, illustrated his point by describing the following event that took place several
years ago:

> The first meeting with these people [the higher Commission officials]
> often occurs during an incident. In my case, I built up trust during the
> handling of a crisis concerning the presence of hormones in animal
> fodder. The Commission proposed destroying all of the animals that
> had been fed the contaminated fodder. ... I told them that we just had
> foot and mouth disease and that a lot of livestock had been destroyed,
> but that this time there was no immediate threat to public health. In

the end, we only had to destroy a far smaller proportion of the animals than initially discussed. I then implemented the decisions carefully and transparently (*Ministry of Agriculture official*).

Ultimately, signalling is applied by both agriculture Eurocrats at the Permanent Representation and the home department. Nurturing networks by national civil servants with Commission officials is a way of institutionalising the signalling strategy. Similar to the situation with private interest lobbies in Brussels, easy and swift access to officials who are co-ordinating or writing the relevant proposals is an important asset for national ministries to cultivate. At the same time, interviewees emphasise that signalling alone is unlikely to do the trick as far as successful uploading is concerned. From the perspective of the national department, i.e., the sender, signalling may appear a relatively cheap and direct strategy, but from the perspective of the receiver (Commission officials) it is bound to be just one of many signals from different sources they receive on a continuous basis. They are not only 'being signalled' by Eurocrats from other member states but also by a range of private interest organisations. When the number of signals from a variety of sources increases, it becomes increasingly difficult for Commission officials to properly assess their relative value. The accumulation of signals may produce a level of 'noise' that may discourage Commission officials from properly scrutinising and assessing the individual signals.

Frontloading proposals
Frontloading aims at exerting direct, substantive influence on the writing of the proposal. Members may obtain direct access to the writing of a Commission proposal by seconding national officials at the targeted Directorate-General. SNEs comprise one of three categories of Commission officials. The first consists of the permanent staff of the Commission services (i.e., grade A officials) who are recruited for the service after having successfully passed their *concours*. The second group consists of support and administrative staff. SNEs, on the other hand, are appointed for fixed periods of time. They are part of the Directorate General and work on a specific file for a period of up to three years. One of the pragmatic reasons for their appointment is that SNEs assist the Commission services staff and bring expertise on issues the Commission lacks knowledge on, or as the official logic of secondments describes it:

Seconded National Experts (SNEs) have a dual role: to bring to the Commission their experience of the issues they are used to dealing with and to take back to their home administration the knowledge of Community issues which they acquire during their secondment. They are seconded in order to let the Commission benefit from the high level of their professional knowledge and experience, in particular in areas where such expertise is not readily available in various fields (EC, http://ec.europa.eu/dgs/personnel_administration/sne_en.htm, 24 July 2006).

Research on seconded national civil servants is sparse, let alone their strategic position and roles. SNEs are often alluded to in European Commission services studies, but have rarely been studied as actors within the EU policy process. Trondal argues that seconded national officials are treated as 'the under-researched "Cinderella" of the Commission' within the academic literature. But in fact they deserve more attention for their function as a 'parallel administration' within the Commission (Trondal 2001). Trondal concludes that 'seconded personnel to the Commission are likely to put particular emphasis on pre-established national and sectoral senses of belonging due to their primary institutional affiliations at the national level of governance' (Trondal 2001: n.p.).

Our interviews with civil servants at the Department of Agriculture and of SNEs in this department shed a somewhat different light on the phenomenon of secondment (see also chapter 5). Although this is often officially denied by the Dutch civil service, the Ministry of Agriculture does strategically second civil servants to Directorates-General of interest to the ministry. The 'official' denial stems from the fact that the Dutch view of the Commission has for a long time been that the Commission is a supranational body that should operate impartially with regard to member states. One of our respondents told us that strategic use of secondment is something the French do, but not the Dutch:

> The French government positions civil servants at the Commission with an assignment. If they fail, it can shake up the rest of their careers. We are less tough but we do have our discussions on this issue (*Ministry of Agriculture official*).

We found that this view is 'on-the-record' policy. Off the record, secondment is perhaps the most important strategic instrument the Dutch Ministry of

Agriculture employs to influence Commission proposals. This is expressed by one of the department's top officials, a director-general:

> The position one [a seconded national official] has is not chosen by co-incidence. It [secondment] is not just [an instrument] for the careers of civil servants. Secondment is of course good for their careers, but the position they occupy is also of importance to the department. They are in a place where we have interests. The places are strategically chosen. You don't give them instructions, but you can do anything you need to do to ensure that they maintain a certain loyalty to the department. But you also deliver a Dutchman to Brussels who will work from a Dutch perspective' (*Ministry of Agriculture official*).

The salience of secondments as a strategic instrument is underlined by the fact that a special working group exists to co-ordinate secondments to the EU and other international organisations that are relevant to the policy areas of agriculture. At the end of the 1990s, the Directorate of International Affairs set up a Working Group for Mobility, headed by the assistant-director of the DIA, to co-ordinate the appointment of SNEs. An interviewee from the working group observed that:

> Within this department we consider international mobility to be very important. We have people in positions who participate in the making of important decisions. They do not deal directly with the Dutch position, but they are placed there strategically, so it is not a coincidence at all. Secondments are strategic (*Ministry of Agriculture official*).

The strategic importance of SNEs is also recognised by the Dutch Food and Consumer Safety Agency (VWA). According to one of its senior officials, the ultimate goal of secondments is indeed the 'pre-cooking' (Larsson 2003) of Commission proposals:

> We [VWA] are in the process of developing outcome-oriented regulatory policies. I do not want our policies to be battered around because the Commission has decided to go for the lowest common denominator. So what I want is for the Commission to start conceiving regulatory policy the way we do it here at the VWA. I'd like to steer the Commission in the direction we are heading ... I have received permission from Agriculture to station two of our [VWA] people at the Food and Veteri-

nary Office in Dublin for a few years ... I think the changes from output to outcome control we have made look very promising. Thus, I try to exert some influence at the source [of the policy process], to in turn exert some influence on the writing side ... (*VWA official*).

The question is: how is this done? How is this strategy executed? It would not be entirely accurate to see the issue of secondments as a one-way street. Reciprocity between international organisations and national governments seems to be a necessary condition for secondments:

> International organisations often want to address a problem, but don't have sufficient manpower at that moment. The deal we make is that we find it interesting as well [*sic*]. We second someone to the organisation and pay all or part of the expenses. They can then begin doing the important work [e.g., against an outbreak of bird flu], that is also important to the Netherlands. This is how we can acquire influence on things that are important to the Netherlands (*Ministry of Agriculture official*).

But this does not imply that the Ministry of Agriculture can freely choose from amongst the available positions:

> The input from the Netherlands should add to the Commission's work. The Netherlands has a good reputation when it comes to cases involving animal diseases and animal welfare. The Netherlands stands a good chance of gaining some positions in these areas if our department decides to lobby for them (*Permanent Representation official*).

Active lobbying involves a good network and preferably personal relationships between Dutch and European officials. 'I know the director of the Food and Veterinary Office very well', one respondent told us, 'and he asked me for personnel. I immediately arranged that' (*VWA official*).

To what extent is this strategy effective in terms of policy outcome? Do seconded civil servants steer the direction of the policy process? Or is the ultimate benefit of having seconded officials within the Commission 'to take the knowledge of Community issues back home' as the official statement of the Commission notes? Seconded national civil servants are expected to be loyal to the Commission and to develop supranational identifications via their frequent interactions with the permanent staff. Some of our respondents are clear about the role of seconded national servants: once they begin in their positions they should be loyal to the Commission and should not be put under pressure by their previous department. At the same time, no respondent denies the benefits that the department accrues from having a seconded official at a strategic position. One benefit is that the parent department can establish a larger network for the entire department through a seconded official:

> We try to encourage the directors of the SNEs to visit them on location. The SNE makes an appointment with his unit head, the director of the unit where he works, and if possible, with the director-general or the vicedirector-general. They first talk about the project, but eventually they end up discussing a whole range of other issues. The purpose of these meetings is to get to know one another. It is much easier to pick up the phone when you know someone personally (*Civil servant at the Ministry of Agriculture*).

The goal is to use the SNE and his or her position to pave the way for high level networks. SNEs are further provided with the basic technical facilities to keep in touch with the parent department. That way they can communicate easily with their colleagues via Internet and via the mail, so that both sides remain informed. The annual securing of The Hague's networks occurs during the 'come back days' when all of the SNEs stationed throughout the many international organisations around the world are invited back for a two-day meeting. SNEs are requested to give seminars on their ongoing affairs. Directors-general are expected to attend these meetings as well. The two-day meeting is concluded by an informal dinner with the directors-general and secretaries-general. The presence of top-level officials sends a signal to the rest of the department that this is an important meeting.

Sometimes, if the events are managed well and the situation allows it, a co-ordinated network of SNEs can lead to the exertion of significant influence on the policy-making process, even as early and as crucial as setting its agenda. One such instance occurred during a crisis management situation involving avian influenza (bird flu) in early March 2006, when a senior Dutch Agriculture official was called upon to attend a meeting at the Food and Agriculture Organisation (FAO) offices:

> I have seconded someone to the FAO for avian influenza, someone to the OIE [Office International des Epizooties] and a couple of people to DG SANCO [the Directorate General for Health and Consumer Af-

fairs]. What happened is that suddenly all of these organisations became preoccupied with the avian influenza situation. Last week I was called to a conference at the FAO to speak about crisis management in cases involving outbreaks of avian influenza. The United States were also invited. There was also someone from OIE, who happened to be a Dutch woman from my directorate who was seconded to the OIE. Another participant in the meeting was a representative from the European Commission, again seconded from my directorate. And finally there was Louise Fresco[24] who was joined by yet another SNE [at FAO] seconded from my directorate. I jokingly proposed 'let's do the meeting in Dutch with an English translator' (*Ministry of Agriculture official*).

The basic impression by the Dutch officials, a majority of whom were SNEs we interviewed, shows that the purposeful and strategic use of seconding may lead to situations where a (small) national state can have a substantial impact on decision-making and agenda setting.

Ethical guidelines notwithstanding, SNEs bring their own national doctrines and their Dutch 'norms and values' to Brussels:

I think that everyone from the Netherlands, whether they are seconded officials or not, approach their work from the perspective of Dutch norms and values. That is very valuable. Therefore, I think that as a member state you can gain influence here if a member state has a lot of officials seconded to the Commission, so that the process in Brussels becomes similar to that of your own country (*SNE*).

This occurred to some extent when the Dutch were invited to second a national civil servant to work on the meat hygiene control dossier. The official was seconded to DG SANCO and worked for three years on the preparation of a proposal for meat hygiene control as part of the General Food Law. The Netherlands has been in favour of developing and implementing a regulatory system whereby hygiene inspections are no longer performed by the state but by the private sector itself. The essence of this system consists of the fact that the Dutch government only assumes 'system responsibilities', remains removed from the actual physical inspection of the slaughterhouses and meat-processing industries, and instead only inspects the systems designed by the private sector itself. The proposal that the Commission submitted to the EP and the Council contained the mode of governance preferred by the Netherlands. 'However', the interviewee explains:

... the European Parliament removed a number of essential issues from the proposal. This can be mainly attributed to the *Rapporteur*. He was a former East German veterinarian with a strong 'statist' perspective. He removed a number of essential issues. The European Parliament's Environment, Public Health and Food Safety Committee rejected some of the *Rapporteur*'s proposals but left others intact. The most essential element of the proposal that did not make it to the final draft was the proposal that slaughterhouses be allowed to control the hygiene of their meat themselves, under the supervision of a veterinarian. The European Parliament preferred that government officials handle this ... The European Parliament's amendments were quite a setback for the Netherlands. It was very inconvenient for this sector because this was the course preferred by the Netherlands (*SNE*).

Despite this, the Ministry of Agriculture and the sector were content to some extent, because the proposals that did survive offered sufficient room for the Netherlands to implement the crucial elements of the preferred course in the Netherlands. This case illustrates that although seconded nationals cannot always forge a preferred position, they can redirect the course of policy development in a specific direction. 'Although our major points were eliminated ... we thought that the end result was a very modern regulation that enabled us to work with the system-level monitoring of meat hygiene' (*Ministry of Agriculture official*).

The above examples should not give the impression that the Commission can simply be manipulated or steered in a desired direction by a national ministry or agency that seconds its civil servants. SNEs are offered opportunities as well as confronted with constraints when they work for their specific departments. Due to the information of seconded officials, national departments are better informed about the positions of other member states and thus oversee potential dilemmas and difficulties of shifting towards a certain of mode of governance. However, the Commission is well aware of the potential dangers inherent in entrusting files to seconded national officials like the seconded respondents we interviewed. SNEs have to operate in a highly political environment where the stakes for the Commission and member states can be very high. An example that illustrates this concerns the dilemma of how to treat confidential information:

When do you give what kind of information to the home front? The Commission produces internal reports of its negotiations. The Commission then says that the reports are internal and we won't share them with the member states. Well, on certain occasions, for example, the Netherlands wants to know the content of a specific report. One thing you can do is to give an oral summary of the report. Going one step further would mean doing this by mail. Or you might just send the entire piece. You can do all this the day after the release of the internal report or a month later. There is an entire grey area of options and what the effects of these options are is dependent on the number of interests that play a role. If the negotiations only concern one country – well, in that case you can inform that member state of what the Commission intends to do. But it changes when several member states, with diverging interests, are involved. If you don't act carefully as a seconded official, or according to the rules of loyalty [which every seconded national official has to agree to upon assuming office] you could end up banging your head against the wall (*SNE*).

Therefore, if the Commission:

> ... has files that ought to remain secret, they give it to that person [a seconded official] to see what happens next. I don't know whether the Commission does this consciously, but they are, of course, not naive (*SNE*).

SNEs are generally 'hired' to work on a specific dossier. As noted earlier, they inevitably bring their own national and professional norms and values to the task, and this is often precisely why the Commission wants a representative of a certain member state to work on a proposal. The moment an SNE enters his or her directorate-general, he or she will inevitably experience a clash of governance modes:

> There was much ado when I was appointed to Brussels. A storm of protest came from Italy because it was fiercely opposed to the Dutch approach regarding meat hygiene controls. They felt that the Netherlands had squandered their meat inspection responsibility by privatising inspections and giving the state only a small role. The Italian CVO [Chief Veterinary Officer] invested a lot of effort in preventing my secondment *(SNE)*.

The secondment could not be prevented, however, but this particular SNE did not have an easy inauguration into Brussels:

> My secondment was looked upon very sceptically, especially by colleagues from Southern Europe. They were very suspicious and critical. My 'patron', a Fleming and the director of my department supported me while my immediate colleagues – most of whom were French or Italian – were the most suspicious. They were sceptical about the Dutch way of thinking regarding meat inspections... However, they had not been instructed by their governments to oppose my work. It was their natural attitude. They have been brought up differently (*SNE*).

To be successful in these circumstances requires a lot from an individual. Our interviewee was fluent in French and Italian and this certainly helped him establish cordial relationships with his colleagues. He also spoke at meetings in Italy on the subject – in Italian – to explain the Dutch approach. And perhaps most of all, 'you have to show that you're not a bad guy' (*SNE*).

In conclusion, we have observed that the use of secondments is a highly preferred and strategic instrument for influencing the content and direction of Commission proposals, but it does not necessarily lead to a successful outcome. Working as a seconded national civil servant is fraught with pitfalls and the Commission is constantly checking the loyalty of its seconded officials.

Coalition formation

The coalition formation strategy typically emerges when representatives of relevant national ministries convene for the first time at a committee meeting. An interviewee gave us an impression of such a meeting, which was concerned with the drafting of a regulation that would control foodstuffs and animal fodder as part of the General Food Law:

> On the basis of a rough draft by the Commission, we [a number of experts from various departments] took a look at the various draft provisions, keeping in mind what the position of the Netherlands should be ... We put our ideas down on paper and went to Brussels and submitted our viewpoint very explicitly ... The meeting began with a round during which each member state presented its views. You immediately pick your potential allies on different issues during this round. You de-

cide on an issue-to-issue basis who your allies will be. The views of the member states remain quite consistent throughout the subsequent committee meetings. So you find yourself in agreement with country A on issue X and with country B on issue Z. Then at the coffee machine you exchange some more ideas in a very informal manner (*Ministry of Agriculture official*).

Prior to a committee meeting, the positions of the other member states on the various issues are often unknown to you. It is even less clear who your potential allies are and what the results of the meetings will be.

A more activist stance is also possible, of course. Interviewees were quick to point out that there are alternatives to letting the outcome of committee meetings be determined by happenstance events. Many of those who regularly travelled back and forth between Brussels and their home base to participate in Commission committees (and Council working groups) on a regular basis stressed the importance of informal discussions 'around the coffee machine' during breaks, after lunches, as well as over drinks and, occasionally, during dinners before or after a meeting.[25] However, these informal circuits are more effective when they are not just limited to committee meetings. One interviewee, who worked on the General Food Law's inspection of hygiene measures, set up and co-ordinated a so-called 'four-country consultation group'. Some time in 2004, during Luxembourg's presidency, German, Dutch, Belgian and Luxembourgian civil servants began meeting on the day before the actual committee meeting in order to discuss the agenda of the upcoming meeting, and to co-ordinate the various issues regarding the import of veterinary products:

During these meetings we look for issues on which we can reach an agreement and where our views diverge. On issues we agree on, we support each other.... and take similar positions. We also discuss tactics: who will say what and when ... At the last committee meeting it went so well that we dominated the meeting ...We had an alliance. What happened then was that none of the newer member states said anything – which is not unusual. But countries like France and the United Kingdom also remained silent. The other countries then apparently figure that 'when Germany, the Netherlands and Belgium already agree' the issue is pretty much settled. We have to be careful with this kind of situation, however. We must not become too dominant and pursue variations. Meaning that we should sometimes openly declare: 'I don't agree with you'. You shouldn't create the impression that the three of us have pre-cooked everything beforehand. I don't think the Commission would be pleased with this state of affairs. But nevertheless we keep going! *(VWA official)*.

The 'consultation' between the four countries and the subsequent 'domination' of the committee meeting – one must admit – occurred during the rather weak Luxembourg Presidency. A small group of member states had managed to 'pre-cook' a position and had presented themselves as a united front vis-à-vis the Commission and the rest of the member states. Under a 'normal' presidency, there is much less room to operate in this fashion and the co-ordination and negotiation costs between the member states are much higher. Nevertheless, this example shows that in a setting with a large number of member states, coalition formation and the pre-cooking of a common position, a small core group of member states can form a front against the Commission and overwhelm the other member states.

This kind of close co-operation between a limited number of member states not only depends on the weaknesses of the presidency but also on the personal relationships between the national Eurocrats involved. In the aforementioned example, the core group often held informal meetings and if this could not take place in a restaurant for financial reasons, they met over home-cooked dinners. Of course this requires a certain level of good personal chemistry.

In a more general sense, the expert committee meetings further impede the strategic actions of member states because of a lack of information regarding the initial positions of the other member states. If you add the complex voting structure to this situation it is not difficult to imagine how difficult it is to determine who will form coalitions with whom, let alone predict the results of the meeting or the Commission's final decision. One further important point should be stressed, however. Our interviews were conducted two years after the EU enlargement. Prior to the enlargement, coalitions in the veterinary field were predictably clustered around the larger member states. Since enlargement, however, agreements within this arena have become much more difficult to predict:

... strategic insight is no longer important. In the old days, the voting blocks were almost always fixed. If the Netherlands was in favour of something, the Italians opposed it. Then if we approached the Germans to support our views and Germany concurred, then the issue was pretty much settled. We just needed to sit back and relax and add nothing. Furthermore, you used to have member states with a certain number of votes so you could make your own calculations. Nowadays, it has become so complex that it is not worth trying to calculate. With twenty-five member states, calculations have become impossible. With which combination of states can you achieve a voting blocking majority? The number of parameters has grown so large that strategic interactions with the representatives of other member states within the committee have become useless. Too many variations are now possible (*VWA official*).

Despite the possibilities for forging small blocks of like-minded countries to dominate the expert committee meetings that pressure the Commission to adopt your positions, this coalition formation strategy is probably less likely to succeed than frontloading plus signalling. Expert groups are established once the Commission has already adopted a direction. It requires a civil servant's networking skills and long-term personal devotion to an issue to invest in coalition formation in order to change the course of a discussion within an expert group toward his country's interests. But the Commission remains in the driver's seat and to a large extent determines the substance of the proposal it submits to the Council and Parliament. Effectively approaching the Commission before it sends something through to various other committees makes perfect sense.

3.5 Eurocratic work as strategic behaviour: Conclusions

This chapter explored the strategic behaviour of national civil servants during the process of uploading departmental preferences at the pre-proposal phase. Not only does it contribute to the research on a relatively unexplored phase of the EU policy process but it also contributes to the study of organisational and individual behaviour at national ministries and among civil servants of the EU member states. It is perhaps one of the first studies on the strategic behaviour of national ministries and civil servants during this crucial phase. If a member state manages to intercede successfully before the Commission initiates a directive or regulation proposal, our theoretical argument proposes, it can impose its preferences on the other member states by influencing the proposal's text. In order for other member states to alter this text and influence the proposal requires the forging of a coalition with a critical mass of other member states during subsequent committee meetings. Given the Commission's powers during this phase and the diffi-culties of forming a successful coalition, the member states that move first actually end up succeeding in locking-in their own positions before the Commission formally submits the proposal to the Council and European Parliament.

This chapter has identified three strategic options based on this logic. Two of these options yield first-mover advantages. The first of these is *signalling*. Signalling was not only considered a major task of Eurocrats at the Permanent Representation, but was also actively employed by their depart-mental counterparts in The Hague. Moreover, not only middle-level civil servants but also the high-ranking civil servants we interviewed reported that they actively contacted and informed Commission officials as an im-portant aspect of their EU-related work.

As regards *frontloading*, secondment turned out to be a highly strategic instrument during the pre-proposal phase, a point that has largely re-mained unexplored in research on SNEs. Existing studies rightly suggest that secondments will affect role perceptions of seconded national officials to some extent and eventually instigate a process of Europeanisation of the culture and social practices at national departments upon their return to their own departments. What has been overlooked, however, is the strategic use of seconded national civil servants in the uploading of national prefer-ences into the EU policy process. In our interviews we found that, more than top-level instructions, the 'natural' national perceptions and outlooks of the seconded national experts were considered as the most important mechanism through which national preferences are translated into Com-mission proposals. Once uploaded and launched into the supranational policy process, the preferences of the member state are usually locked into the highly institutionalised policy process at this level.

Finally, the findings we presented on the *coalition formation* strategy of member states during the proposal formation phase underscore the find-ings in the literature thus far. The Commission has extensive formal and in-formal powers during the pre-proposal phase; it not only has the right to ini-tiate a proposal but also the capacities to steer and shape the committee deliberation process during the pre-proposal phase. The increased number of member states and increased complexity of voting influence among the member states within the Council working groups during the subsequent decision-making phase have made it almost impossible for member states to operate strategically during the proposal-formation phase. Thus, the only successful case we noted is, in a sense, exceptional: the co-ordination of national positions among the four countries occurred in one specific area during a weak presidency. Like in the case of signalling, individual civil servants are 'alone out there' when negotiating with their counterparts from other member states. Furthermore, they need to know how the game is played and must have sufficient knowledge and expertise to earn the necessary standing and reputation.

CHAPTER 4

GETTING THINGS DONE IN EUROPEAN POLICE CO-OPERATION

'I am here to represent the Netherlands, and my colleagues back home sometimes find it difficult to appreciate that. They do the bidding of the individual ministries. Their arena is about pulling and hauling between ministries. Here the arena is about pulling and hauling between countries' (Official of the Dutch Permanent Representation in the EU).

Q: Are you a Dutchman, a European, or a Euregional citizen?
'I am first and foremost a Euregional policeman. As far as my organisational back office is concerned, I am embedded in the Dutch system, but the actual job lies in this transnational region, and this is on the increase. So I have to play chess simultaneously on two boards: the Dutch and the Euregional. That implies an additional work load.'
Q: Do you behave differently because of this?
'There is no hierarchy in the co-operation with the other countries. It is more a social, network-like thing. Co-operation is all you've got. It is much less direct than working in a national command hierarchy. You actually have to place yourself in the other person's shoes' (A senior police official in the Dutch province of Limburg).

4.1 Eurocratic work in the Third Pillar: A different world?

In this chapter, as in the previous one, we will look at European governance through the eyes of people who routinely 'do it' as part of their jobs as national civil servants. We want to know how these national Eurocrats operate in international arenas and how this EU-related work is embedded in and facilitated by the organisations they are part of. In chapter 3, we focused on the veterinary policy case, in which the Commission was a crucial actor, driving a highly institutionalised regime of technocratic deliberation and negotiation, which is punctuated only occasionally by politically explosive issues such as BSE and avian influenza. We demonstrated that, in this context, Eurocratic work evolves around a number of key tactics (signalling, frontloading and coalition formation) that allow the main actors to gain and maintain control of the course and outcomes of key dossiers.

In the current chapter, we switch our focus to study Dutch Eurocrats in the field of European police co-operation. They are mainly employed either by the Ministries of the Interior and Justice, by the 25 regional police forces, or by the single national police force; some of them are stationed at the Dutch Permanent Representation in Brussels or at organisations like Europol. Police co-operation is – to a large extent – a Third Pillar issue area, which means that it is governed by a much less developed regime of collective transnational decision-making than a First Pillar area like veterinary policy. We suspect that this arena may offer national Eurocrats different types of incentives for 'getting things done' than those afforded to their veterinary counterparts.

The quotes cited above illustrate what we would like to argue here: that the role orientations and rules of thumb the officials who work on police co-operation have developed in the course of their European experiences vary markedly. They 'do business in Europe' in very different ways. Depending on the issue area and its 'rules of the game,' national Eurocrats operate in very different kinds of policy networks at the European level. Grasping these various logics is pivotal to understanding what it takes to operate at the nexus between national and transnational policy-making.

4.2 The case of data availability: 'Messy' policy-making in Europe

Data availability is a hot topic at the various European Justice and Home Affairs institutions. The transnational sharing of information on anything – people, communication data, (stolen) vehicles, arms, explosives, poison, money – that may lead to safety or security threats among the member states is considered vital by all of the governments involved. Yet plans to facilitate this information sharing have aroused serious privacy concerns, fears about a loss of sovereignty in this key domain of state activity, as well as charges that these measures may undermine the rule of law. Different national viewpoints on data-sharing have surfaced repeatedly in the preparations for the Council of JHA Ministers, and as such, this case provides us with a poignant view of how Dutch Eurocrats deal with such a hot topic. Below we present our observations and interviews in several arenas where this issue gets processed and plays out in terms of both policy-making and implementation.

An expert committee: Working Party on Police Co-operation

On 25 January 2006, a meeting was held at the Dutch Ministry of the Interior in The Hague. Its purpose was to prepare the Dutch position on a proposal from the Austrian Presidency for a Council decision on improving police co-operation between EU member states. A major part of the proposal concerned procedures for improving transnational information sharing among police forces. The head of the Dutch delegation had to present the Dutch position on the proposal a day later, during a meeting of the Police Co-operation Working Party, one of the countless committees that prepare and help implement European policies and programmes. He was a senior official at the Interior Ministry and was chairing the discussion. In attendance were four of his counterparts from the Ministry of Justice (the Ministries of the Interior and Justice share responsibility for Dutch policing policy). There were also two representatives from the Dutch National Police, both veterans who had seen their last operational action years ago.

They discussed the technical aspects of the Austrian proposal: could the Dutch police departments meet the requirements envisaged in the proposal, would they have to adjust their information systems, and could one expect the police forces of other member states to do likewise? The relevant treaties which might bear upon the proposed measures were presented. No mention was made of ministerial or parliamentary decisions or opinions on the subject. There was no real debate about anything on the agenda and the participants seemed to agree on the issues, with the 'Dutch position' simply emerging from that consensus. Some of the policemen present did not seem to be fully aware of the European procedural 'nitty-gritty' involved in European policy-making. They inquired about the European Parliament's role. One of the Justice Department civil servants suggested in a condescending manner that they attend 'a course on European matters' to be offered soon.

The meeting of the Police Co-operation Working Party took place in Brussels the next day on 26 January. The meeting was an all-day affair in the same enormous conference room where the Justice and Home Affairs (JHA) Council of Ministers meets, the eventual 'end station' for all these preparatory meetings. Every participant could speak in his or her native language with interpreters available. All of the participants wore earphones throughout the meeting. Film cameras were an essential part of the interaction process because everyone had their own screen on their desks with each speaker in close up, for everyone to read his or her every facial expression. There were also several enormous screens projecting the same images. The Dutch delegation was small; besides the delegation leader there was also an official from the Dutch Permanent Representation to the EU. The most striking aspect of the meeting ritual was that participants were referred to not by their own names, but by their country's. Every participant was seated around a large oval table, behind a sign which bore the country's name. When a participant wanted to speak the chairperson would grant him or her permission, by declaring: 'The Netherlands, the floor is yours', and would wrap up the Dutch presentation with words like 'Thank you, the Netherlands'. Another striking thing was how little contact there was between the representatives of the different delegations. Everybody was polite but reserved. There were very few informal greetings or casual asides. Participants were also very formal toward the chair. The Presidency had just changed hands, as it does every six months in the EU. And so, each of the speakers prefaced his or her opening remarks by formally wishing the Austrian chair well with their presidency and expressing their intention to fully co-operate. The politeness was reciprocal as all of the participants had found small gifts at their desk when arriving in the conference room, bureaucratic gifts like a tie or a booklet with the logo of the new presidency on it.

Furthermore, there was no sign of the much-vaunted Brussels lunching-cum-lobbying circuit. The Dutch delegation had a simple lunch together at the Salle Bleu, one of the restaurants in the building. The head of the delegation finished his lunch before the others to have a talk with the Irish delegation on a project the Irish had proposed, which partly overlapped with a Dutch proposal that was also up for discussion. He also made a phone call to The Hague to one of his colleagues.

During the meeting, the various proposals on the agenda were discussed in depth. It was a long day with arcane technical matters receiving much of the attention. The key proposal had been discussed before in other Council working groups like ENFOPOL, ENFOCUSTOM, CRIMORG and COMIX. Remarkably, almost no one referred to these earlier discussions; it was as if the participants had never been briefed on these other meetings.

Meanwhile, the Austrian chair tried to reach agreements on as many aspects of the proposal as possible. The meeting was mostly about gauging, shaping and bending words until everybody could agree. By the end of the discussion, the chair offered a short summary of the suggested proposal changes. She also summed up the issues for which no consensus had been reached. The proposal was now forwarded to next week's *Comité de l'Article Trente-Six* (CATS), another co-ordinating committee of more senior civil servants. CATS would zoom in on those parts of the proposal on which no consensus had been reached. These parts were now referred to as the more 'political' parts of the proposal. Apparently, they were not 'technical', for no consensus had been reached. After CATS had been fully discussed, perhaps modified and signed off on the proposal, it was then sent further up the European policy-making hierarchy, to the *Comité de Représentants Permanents* (COREPER), the meeting of the EU ambassadors of the member states. Once it was approved there, the proposal would end up being voted on in the JHA Council of Ministers.

A high-level committee: CATS

The Ministry of Justice official who was formerly at the Permanent Representation in Brussels and who had participated in the preparation of the CATS committee indicated that he was acutely aware of the disjointed nature of the working group system. He thought the European Commission actually exploits the 'organised anarchy' in the Third Pillar by offering its proposals to different working groups, hoping that at least one of these channels will end up directing this proposal to the Council. However, the leader of the Dutch delegation to the CATS committee disagreed that the Commission was playing the system. He thought it would be a great improvement if all proposals to the Council in the Third Pillar could be made by the Commission. This would at least bring some consistency to the messiness with one actor who can maintain an overview of the entire process. This is currently not the case. His chief concern with the current system was that political pressures might lead the high-level actors in the CATS and JHA to approve a hastily patched-together proposal that comes out of 'nowhere.' According to him, 'the culture of the European arena is such that any decision is considered better than no decision at all'. He deplored the *ad-hocracy* this tended to produce, citing instances in which decisions clearly conflicted with prior CATS decisions, or with a decision made by another forum in the JHA.

The head of the Dutch delegation also noted that there was another form of pressure in the CATS committee process. At the end of the day, the CATS participants are accountable to their own national bureaucratic constituencies. Thus they each keep one key criterion in mind: is there something in it for 'us'? The bottom line of the CATS meetings is that all of the participants are first and foremost national civil servants, and feel compelled to act as such – or face uncomfortable questions back home.

The CATS delegation leaders identify themselves first and foremost as national civil servants, at least as much as the participants in the Working Party on Police Co-operation described earlier, even though they seem to know each other better than their lower-level counterparts do, addressing each other (by way of the chairperson) by their first names during the meeting. The Dutch delegation leader said that he himself would like to act more as a genuine 'European', taking the common good instead of the Dutch interest as his reference point for judging proposals and taking positions. Unfortunately, he said, his colleagues in The Hague, as well as his counterparts in forums such as CATS are overwhelmingly locked into their national perspectives and seem primarily intent on preserving their existing national policies, procedures and judicial systems. He welcomed the pressure put on his colleagues by the Foreign Ministry and Permanent Representation, 'who regularly argue that something has to happen, some improvements have to be made. If it weren't for that, everybody would simply lie back and wait.'

A member of the Permanent Representation confirms this point of view: 'There is very little vision on which way to head in police co-operation. The general idea is to try to avoid inconveniences brought on by anything new. It would be so much better to try and benefit from new initiatives.' A colleague from the Ministry of the Interior hints at why civil servants seem to act the way they do: 'As long as there is no clear political vision regarding a certain theme, there is not much vision developed among civil servants either. We stick to the political vision.' This, he said, breeds conservatism: 'We are against a proposal because we have always been against it even if no one knows any more what exactly was the reason for taking that position.'

The CATS delegation leader considered himself lucky to have a 'European-minded' minister. This gave him a lot of support in urging his colleagues to 'get on with it'. The Dutch Minister for Justice had made crime-fighting his top priority and was strongly aware of its European dimension. After the CATS meeting, the delegation leader pointed out that this provided him with opportunities. 'Within the Netherlands, you often act as the representative of an EU position: you overact your European allegiance in order to create room to manoeuvre. You do the reverse in Brussels, by saying: "I cannot possibly take this back to my superiors at home."'

An operational arena: Europol

As far as data availability is concerned, it is all about trust, according to many policemen – as it is indeed the case in other areas of European police co-operation as well. Even if police officers are aware of the necessity of international collaboration in the fighting of crime, they will not necessarily share information with their foreign colleagues. They cite various reasons. First, professional jealousy: 'Why should we allow others to show off in cracking cases that we did all the work on?' Second, reputation: 'Who knows what police departments in "funny" countries will do with our information?' The new member states especially are treated with considerable caution. Most policemen we spoke with cite this as the main reason why any EU decisions on making data available to police forces from states other than a carefully selected batch of trusted ones would prove difficult to implement – even when the political pressure to comply is enormous. A case in point is Europol, a Europe-wide agency specifically set up to advance transnational information sharing and police co-operation. Politicians and high-ranking civil servants wanted to create a central data system to analyse key criminal and terrorist threats. In practice, police departments in most member states deliver too little data too late for the system to get up and running. 'They just don't do it,' observed a recently retired Dutch policeman who had spent years at Europol, and 'this is a source of enormous frustration to the management board of Europol.'

The bumpy road of Europol's efforts to advance information sharing and its own stifled institutional development testify to an iron law of police co-operation: police officers need to feel an operational urgency (and payoff) to co-operate, and to be able to trust one another. If one of these is so much as ambiguous, they won't move – whatever is being decided in Brussels and national capitals. This is worsened by practices at Europol's Management Board. There has been little interest in Europol among the Dutch police; it is only recently that one of the regional police chiefs took up the task of representing the Dutch police force at Europol's Management Board. The chair of the Dutch delegation is the head of a department at the Ministry of Justice. By way of an example, we recount the second day of a two-day meeting of Europol's Management Board in The Hague. It started at 10:00 a.m. with a closed session on who should be formally proposed to the JHA Council as a replacement for one of the deputy directors of Europol. Only delegation leaders were allowed into the conference room. The rest of the delegation members were waiting outside in the lounge. The Dutch delegation had four members waiting outside. At 11:30 there was a coffee break and the delegation leader mentioned that the discussion regarding the first candidate of three was still going on. Representatives of some member states were quarrelling despite intensive diplomacy and agreements earlier. At 13:00, there was another break, now for lunch. Discussion began again at 14:00 and finally at 15:00 the closed session was finished. As was noted by one of the delegation members during the closed session, after about half an hour, some participants were already beginning to leave the meeting in order to be able to catch their planes at Schiphol airport to be able to get back home that same day. At 17:00, when the chair finally wanted to discuss and confirm the minutes of the last meeting, there were not enough participants left to have a quorum.

Co-operation on the ground: Euregional policing

Yet another transnational site where data availability is considered to be pivotal is in the so-called 'Euregions': border areas where, for example, police officials from the Netherlands, Belgium and Germany collaborate closely to combat transborder organised crime. These policemen are in the thick of that fight and they consider the sharing of information about criminals and criminal acts with their foreign colleagues essential to making any headway. They don't care about legal niceties, they want workable procedures. They are convinced that it is impossible to design these for 25 member states simultaneously, as the working group meeting attendees often attempt to do. Instead, they have formed 'experimental' multinational teams with their neighbouring colleagues to find out what is possible, legally speaking, and what works for them. They have formed units like the Bureau of Euregional Co-operation in Maastricht in which the judicial base for this co-operation is laid out and a unit called Epic in which police representatives from the above-noted three countries work to accommodate information requests from their partners.

Epic is located in Heerlen, a city near Maastricht. It is a pretty unique situation. There is no fixed hierarchical structure. The rules of the game evolve as they go along. Representatives from Belgium, Germany and the Netherlands sit around large round tables in mixed groups with computer screens in front of them. Instead of formally processing information requests, they just ask for the necessary information across the table. Legal experts are available to handle the requests for legal assistance from other countries.

The linguistic mechanics of making it work are fascinating. The Dutch in Limburg, located in the southern part of the country, speak a dialect that resembles German. The Dutch, German and Flemish-speaking Belgian policemen communicate with each other in German or Dutch dialect. The French-speaking Belgians are mostly assisted by the Flemish-speaking Belgians, or by some of the Dutch who speak French.

One of the Dutch policemen who initiated the Euregional Bureau observed that the key ingredients for its successful launch were: practical crime-fighting expertise, personal relationships, intercultural respect, a sense of urgency to make a difference in tackling universally abhorred crimes such as child pornography, and the ability to align working methods across borders. Seen from up close, Epic's everyday practices are still quite mundane. About 80 % of its work remains confined to responding to simple requests like identifying car owners by checking licence plates. Moreover, cops from one country are not legally allowed to search each other's data systems. Once this changes, Epic must gear up to the much more complicated task of not only rapidly delivering information on request, but also analysing the available information in the more than 90 data banks it can then access. Its current staff – mostly officers who have left operational service because of one issue or another – is hardly up to that. But the ambition is clearly there, as is the knowledge that the current political mood – information sharing is widely advocated as a pivotal component in the 'wars' on crime and terrorism – is ticking in Epic's favour.

4.3 Species of Eurocrats

The case of data availability illustrates that 'European governance' or 'Europeanised policy-making' is produced in a series of loosely coupled arenas, whose participants are not necessarily aware of their counterparts' existence, postures and decisions. Nor are they always well-informed about the bigger institutional configuration in which these are embedded. Working on European data availability and police co-operation mobilises very different sorts of national civil servants driven by different rationales, operating in different 'European' arenas, often with considerable discretion, employing different notions of the 'rules of the game' in 'doing police co-operation'.

The data availability case and many others like it suggest that conventional accounts describing it as 'governing by committee' (Christiansen and Kirchner 2000) and 'expertocracy', where policies are crafted by 'epistemic communities' of experts (Haas 1992) are only partially correct. It would be more accurate to describe EU governance as evolving through multiple, loosely coupled, multi-level networks (cf. Egeberg, Schaeffer and Trondal 2003).

EU working groups and committees certainly constitute focal points for crafting European policies. They are multinational settings in which national civil servants operate as both policy experts and representatives of their countries, and in that way, as the new diplomats mentioned in chapter 1. Although the policies they agree on are post-national in the sense that these are more than just piling up national policies and regulations, the policy process through which they arrive at this is multinational (Thedvall 2006). Although working groups and committees are often said to be about experts talking to experts, our observations and interviews in this case in the intergovernmental setting of the Third Pillar strongly suggest that they still are first and foremost about countries talking to countries, through their representatives.

The multinational perspective is being reinforced by the rituals that are performed during the meetings. As we saw, for example, participants are referred to not by their own names but by their country's. Some representatives seek coalitions with others in order to get the meeting to adopt the policies or regulations they prefer. This is not only done during the official meetings, but also during lunches, dinners and coffee breaks: these constitute the backstage of European committee governance, which is much more intense in First Pillar affairs than in the Third Pillar. Sometimes representatives get together in the evening before the meeting with the intention of preparing for the meeting and forming allegiances. Sometimes they sound one another out by e-mail or telephone calls prior to the meetings.

The national outlook of Eurocrats dominates not only their encounters with their counterparts in working groups and committees; it also governs their relations with the primary representatives of a post-national logic of European policy-making: Commission officials. Representatives of member states come in with a focus on their national interests and somehow have to arrive at post-national policies through deliberative and negotiating processes. This can be time-consuming, and the compromises and package deals that emerge from it may produce watered down policies that satisfy no-one. The Commission wants to maintain speed and focus in the policy-making process by intervening in the discussions in working groups and delivering a steady stream of post-national proposals, which representatives of member states in this setting time and again interpret as attempts to control their national affairs.

National Eurocrats experience a dilemma in these situations. Some of our Dutch interviewees expressed a sense of despair at the predictable and stifling way in which all representatives of member states seem to only want to agree upon policies that fit their national systems. They detest the 'conservatism' that it breeds, as one of them labelled it. However, at the same time, they remain trapped in doing exactly the same thing themselves. At the end of the day, they too define their professional success in terms of getting their national positions passed – and at the very least of preventing them from being disregarded altogether. After all, this is what they are held accountable for by their peers and in their national back offices. And so they too display a reluctance to embrace truly post-national solutions, and play the tedious game of multinational bargaining instead.

So far so good. But to leave it like this would obscure as much as it reveals about how Dutch officials do their European business. The various Dutch policing Eurocrats we studied were engaged in rather different types of international transactions. The nature of what it was they co-operated on across borders seemed to reflect the kinds of transnational network arrangements in which they did so.

Bureaucrat-diplomats
Take the data availability issue that was just presented above. The Brussels Working Party on Police Co-operation and the CATS committee represent what we could call bureaucratic-diplomatic arenas of making European policy. The craft of the Eurocrats that populate these arenas revolves around two stages: first, as bureaucrats at home, they need to construct a national position out of often heterogeneous sets of views and preferences of various (sub-)departmental and other stakeholders (i.e., the police), often without any clear political positions steering them; then, as diplomats, they need to represent and defend those national positions whilst bargaining with representatives from other member states. To some this is simple stuff. One Ministry of Justice official boasted:

> Working in EU settings is actually very straightforward. Everybody knows this but it is rarely ever said aloud. When you go to Brussels you say to your colleagues at home: 'It will be tough to achieve this.' When you are in Brussels you tell your fellow committee members: 'I must be able to sell this at home.' And so you always have an explanation for the result you achieve.

The bureaucratic-diplomatic view of Eurocratic work corresponds closely to the traditional picture of the EU as a multilevel system of committee governance. We found it to be prevalent among two groups of Dutch officials.

Firstly, among ministry officials of the kind called 'policy bureaucrats' by Page and Jenkins (2005): academically-trained professionals charged with policy development and maintenance in particular issue areas. Their involvement in European policy processes flows from their portfolio responsibilities and is issue-based, sporadic and often does not constitute a major part of their working week. They are not specifically interested in EU institutions and processes, nor have they received any formal training in their modus operandi. They are just 'following their dossiers' to preparatory meetings within and between Dutch ministries, and occasionally to expert or working group meetings in Brussels. To many, acting on the European stage may be a regular, but quite often an infrequent, part of their jobs. Nor is it necessarily the most important part of their jobs. Much depends, as always, on the priority given to the topic by the departmental hierarchy.

In many cases, these policy bureaucrats are not particularly well-prepared for the new world they are about to enter when they are first assigned EU-related tasks. We cite two voices from a much bigger chorus:

> They just let you go to Brussels. It isn't a very structured thing. You just go there and begin to operate. You learn by doing, and by observing others doing it.

And:

> I stumbled into the European scene in 1985 because my portfolio required me to attend meetings in Brussels. Your older colleagues or your head of unit would give you some coaching. They would come with you once or twice and after that it was 'you're on your own now – good luck with it.'

Some of these officials may continue to be charged with European portfolios for long periods of time. In the organisations studied, this was far more likely to happen to officials at the Agriculture and Justice Ministries than to their colleagues at the Interior and Health Ministries. Those that do build up considerable experience in the do's and don'ts of operating in Brussels. Taken together, this constitutes a potentially valuable body of rules of thumb and 'survival techniques' that does not seem to get codified and transmitted systematically from EU veterans to EU novices within the various departments. People are sent to courses at the Dutch Institute of International Affairs (Clingendael) or the National Government Training Institute (ROI). This is deemed useful by many to get a grip on the institutional framework of the EU, learn about intercultural negotiation and so on. Such formal training remains useful even for those with hands-on experience, as one official confirmed:

> After two years on the Brussels circuit I went to the Dutch Institute of International Affairs to do a course. It was interesting to finally get the bigger picture about the entire EU project – how all the pieces of the puzzle are supposed to fit. If you are only attending committee meetings you don't grasp this at all.

The second group which practices and espouses the bureaucratic-diplomatic view of Eurocratic work are the 'EU insiders': EU co-ordinators at ministries, officials attached to the Permanent Representation, and high-level officials who chair delegations at high-level meetings. For all the differences between their 'average working days', all of these people describe their work as proceeding in a more-or-less scripted, predictable fashion. Theirs is the world of institutionalised bargaining – both at home and in multilateral forums. In that world, which they regard as not very unlike that of other multilateral institutions such as the UN or the WTO, the scope of the possible is determined by existing treaties, agreements and regulatory frameworks, as well as by balances of power, veto players and coalitions. Knowledge about these things tends to be widely shared among the participants, all socialised over time to become EU insiders.

Being effective in this world, these civil servants maintain, requires astute anticipation of the institutional balance between Council, Commission, Parliament and member states. Preparatory work may also involve 'massaging' key gatekeepers within EU institutions, particularly Commission policy bureaucrats who are shaping the proposals, but also pivotal MEPs. More generally, it requires smart 'venue shopping' within these constituent forces: talking to the right people in the right bodies at the right time in the right way. The actual EU working group, committee and Council meetings are seen as pivotal occasions for bargaining and issue-by-issue coalition building that build on this preparatory work. Those who do their homework well ought not to be surprised by what transpires there, and they should be well-placed to shape their decision-making processes, if only by short-circuiting them in advance (as became clear in some of the examples we gave above). By virtue of their institutional and tactical know-how, EU insiders are ideally able to foresee how particular issues will play out, and take timely action to steer the process in desired directions. However, the sheer complexity of the processes involved makes the fool-proof prediction and control of the policy process difficult to achieve.

Departmental co-ordination bureaucrats
In the domestic 'back office' of EU policy-making, Eurocratic work boils down to aligning departmental and interdepartmental policy co-ordination to the rhythms, procedures and routines of scheduled EU meetings. In these preparatory meetings, 'the national interest', and therefore the 'national position' on any given topic on the EU agenda, gets defined. Civil servants attending these preparatory meetings formulate what the national interest is, often in the absence of clearly articulated ministerial preferences, let alone cabinet policy. They are flying blindly quite a lot of the time.

On touchy topics like data availability and information sharing in the criminal justice field, ministers do formulate opinions, but on politically less salient issues, civil servants at the meeting construct a 'national perspective' all by themselves. They brief Dutch delegation leaders in the working group or committee in Brussels on these positions. Delegation leaders then make their own judgements on how to interpret the instruction; they know full well that much of what The Hague feeds them does not come straight from the top, and thus can be taken with a grain of salt.

Discretion is the name of the game in this process. A representative in the Multidisciplinary Working Group on Organised Crime observed:

> Often it is individuals themselves who determine the national position. I think that is weird. If something does not have a fire-alarm character or very high priority you can decide yourself what to do. [The delegation leader] does that a lot of the time. But he also discusses it. When he decided to no longer defend a certain position in CATS, he came by to tell me. That was a unique occasion. Generally you never hear about anything again ... In the international arena, your autonomy is bigger than in the national arena. That is because it has less priority. The national and the international are completely separated.

A Head of Delegation to one of the committees echoed this observation:

> You must know your instructions well, but you should also know the entire process that produced the instructions in order to gauge the weight of the various interests involved. You try to achieve your in-

structions, and if that's impossible, you try to at least achieve its bottom line. However, the instructions are often useless, frankly. The official who actually attends the working group knows its dynamics best. You must not lose out on the really vital issues. You have a lot of discretion, but you must of course anticipate The Hague's reactions.

The co-ordinators at ministries are at the hub of this process of defining positions, drafting instructions and monitoring outcomes. As one puts it:

Most EU dossiers touch upon the work of two or more parts of this ministry: the EU's way of dividing up policy issues does not correspond perfectly with the Dutch departmental division of labour. There is a need for a 'sorting station'. That's what we do.

In some ministries (Justice, Agriculture) these units provide a comprehensive, centralised system of co-ordinating EU policy matters across the full range of the ministry's portfolio. Others, such as the Ministry of the Interior, have opted for a more hybridised system where a central co-ordination unit focuses on procedural matters, whereas the international units of the policy or executive sections deal more closely with the substantive preparation of meetings in specific issue areas (such as policing and intelligence). Meanwhile, others, such as the Ministry of Health, have no such co-ordination unit at all. The domestic EU affairs co-ordinators we encountered seem to agree that two things are particularly important in their jobs. The first is getting those that matter in one's own department to grant appropriate priority to the issues. This may be an uphill struggle, however. In the four ministries examined here, differences in ministerial involvement were marked: low, passive and almost non-existent in Health and Interior; the opposite in Agriculture and Justice. When ministers have other priorities, the ministry's top officials tend to have the same priorities.

The second part of a co-ordinator's job is to develop a clearly articulated departmental position on any given issue, and make sure this position carries weight in interdepartmental co-ordination processes prior to EU meetings. Bureaucratic politics does not stop at the border and the domestic co-ordination of EU policy is a well-known bureaucratic battleground in many countries (Kassim et al. 2000). The Netherlands is certainly no exception to this rule; its ministries are large and internally heterogeneous; 'joined-up government' has proven an elusive ideal at best; and the machinery of interdepartmental co-ordination of EU affairs has been the subject of repeated investigations, discussions and tugs of war between the Foreign Ministry and the Prime Minister's office.

The run-up to high-level European meetings are like any other policy issue of significance and rife with interdepartmental scuffles:

> We at the Ministry of the Interior often prepare texts to be delivered by our minister at the JHA Council. Sometimes our minister decides not to attend the meeting because of time constraints when some of the decisions are in the domain of the Ministry of the Interior. Instead, he leaves it up to the Minister of Justice to represent us. The Minister of Justice always does a very good job. He is very much internationally oriented, and communicates well with his foreign colleagues. But it ultimately weakens the position of the Ministry of the Interior vis-à-vis the Ministry of Justice.

Those who sit in the hot seat as delegation leaders in Brussels obviously have leverage over the other departments and other stakeholders whose interests are at stake in these meetings. That is why interdepartmental sensitivities like the one mentioned above develop. Ministries with top-ranking officers who do not give high priority to European issues tend to be on the losing end of the interdepartmental scuffles. It is hard for the EU co-ordinators in these ministries to get their organisation's voice heard in the interdepartmental preparations for EU meetings. They lack their own 'prize fighters' who can be brought into the ring when other departments attempt to usurp power, e.g., by securing Head of Delegation spots in crucial EU committees and working groups, and by dominating the crafting of Dutch positions on important issues.

'Street-level' entrepreneurs
How different is the world of the other kinds of Eurocrats we encountered. In general, they were people whose main orientation is their own profession, whose natural habitat is the operational practices in the field (i.e., 'street-level'), and whose main drive is to have themselves heard on the international/European stage, ultimately to solve the practical problems they encountered in these practices in whichever way that works.

The function of Eurocrats is experienced quite differently by those who work in the Euregional Bureau. The employees there have an entrepreneurial perspective, which involves forging street-level co-operation to solve pressing problems in public service delivery. Entrepreneurial Eurocrats focus on the establishment of transborder investigations, enforcement measures and officer training programmes.

The dichotomy of national versus post-national identities (with traces of departmental identities) that bureaucrat-diplomats struggle with does not fully capture the role orientation of these operational practitioners because they are, above all, experts in their field. Technical knowledge and professional skills are their stock-in-trade, and form the primary lens through which they view and assess their foreign counterparts and the possibilities for co-operative ventures. Combining an expert's knowledge with a zealot's drive in a context of at best embryonic European institutions and policies that circumscribe and define what needs to be done and how can go a long way toward helping a national Eurocrat shape specific policies with a small group of kindred spirits. When we asked Police Commissioner Ad Hellemons, Director of European Affairs of the Transport Police Division of the Dutch National Police Agency, to describe a 'typical working day on the European circuit' he picked a particular day and recounted:

My alarm clock goes off at 3 a.m. I live in the western part of Brabant (in the southwestern region of the Netherlands) and can hop in and out of Paris in a day. I am in my car half an hour later and arrive in Paris in time to beat the rush hour. I reach the Gendarmerie's headquarters well in time to share a coffee with the officers on duty in the General's secretariat. I know them from previous encounters and, since I am reasonably fluent in French, I can chat a bit with them to get a sense of the day's mood. I visit the French to get them to commit to certain new TISPOL [see box] initiatives. I helped found TISPOL and was president of it for many years. When I arrive I know that my immediate counterpart in the French traffic police division is already on board, but French hierarchy requires that the matter be taken up by the very top before anything can happen. I know I have to begin my conversation with the General in such a way as to enable him to conduct himself in French without having to draw attention to his limited fluency in English. That hurdle taken, we make some small talk. Then I gently steer the conversation toward the topic at hand. I stress the pivotal importance of French 'leadership', you know, the stuff he likes to hear. In fact, it is not all that difficult to get people like the General to co-operate. They know I am not a loose cannon. TISPOL has a good reputation because, since its inception, the number of road deaths in Europe has been falling dramatically. An hour later, my business is done. I hit the road and I'm back home in the early afternoon.

Hellemons epitomises the ideal type of 'other Eurocrat': the doers, the experimenters, the rule-benders, the venue-shoppers. People like him have been the most conspicuous in the police co-operation field, which consists of police commissioners and public prosecutors in areas along the borders, narcotics and road safety specialists and police educators. The open, not yet highly institutionalised, non-supranational structure of Third Pillar policy-making invites this kind of behaviour. Officials of this ilk are mainly people driven to reduce transborder threats to safety affecting day-to-day operations of their police forces, issues they could not possibly tackle all by themselves. They need information and collaboration from foreign colleagues to enable them to do their core business. Unlike the bureaucrat-diplomats in

---

TISPOL Mission Statement

The TISPOL Organisation has been established by the traffic police forces of Europe in order to improve road safety and law enforcement on European roads. Our main priority is to reduce the number of people being killed and seriously injured on Europe's roads. We believe the enforcement of traffic law and education, where appropriate, will make a significant contribution to reducing the carnage on our roads. This is evident in a number of TISPOL member countries.

The objectives of TISPOL

1. To reduce road deaths and casualties on European Roads.
2. To bring together the Roads and Traffic Police Forces in Europe to work together and exchange best practices.
3. Organising and co-ordinating pan-European operations and campaigns.
4. To encourage enforcement and education based on research, intelligence and information so as to establish an effective and targeted education and enforcement programme.
5. Initiating and supporting research on road safety.
6. Providing an informed and co-ordinated police opinion on road safety issues.

Source: www.tispol.org/about

ministerial back offices and at the Permanent Representation, co-operation for them is a means to a clear end rather than a generic, ongoing task of managing Dutch participation in the EU committee system and working groups.

TISPOL is the focus of Ad Hellemons' Eurocratic entrepreneurship and has been by all accounts very successful. He explained how this came to pass:

The problem of transportation policing in Europe is that roads and mobility policy is made by our cousins in the First Pillar, whereas our family inhabits the Third Pillar. This implies that the policy and rules the transport police are supposed to enforce are made in the First Pillar, without any participation by the enforcers. That Third Pillar is a monstrosity because of its unanimity rule and a serious lack of interest in policing matters. If it is not about terrorism or organised crime, they tend to ignore it, but the reality is that no less than 30% of police officers' available time in Europe is involved in traffic one way or another. Contact between the First and Third pillar on this issue is non-existent. When decisions are made in your absence, all that is left for you to do as a police organisation is to clear up the mess afterwards, for instance, having to enforce policies that are basically unenforceable or downright self-defeating. The activities of these two pillars should be linked, but that wasn't happening. And so we as representatives of the traffic police forces have drawn an arrow from the Third to the First Pillar. That arrow constitutes my role orientation ... we have set up three different networks, but the largest and most developed of them is TISPOL. It has members from all of the EU states on board as well as several candidate states and Switzerland and Norway. It is fully financed by First Pillar money ... for me it means a lot of driving. Trips like the one to Paris. They are about making contact, looking the other guy in the eye and using old contacts as stepping stones for making new ones. This network has now been established and is fully financed by the Commission. It is officially a British foundation and we have a president, financial director and an executive board. I am the executive director. The owners are comprised of all the participating police forces. We have five working groups for exchanging information, developing joint training programs, developing pilot projects and reporting systems, and planning joint operations. We are quite operational. We run 50 to 60 pan-European enforcement operations per year... To fund various projects, we compete for Commission money by submitting proposals. We maintain good contacts with Commission officials and have had about 19 of our proposals funded.

Q: *How did you get into the Commission with this project?*

It's very simple, you check on the Web who is dealing with traffic safety issues and you walk in. To give you an idea, there are only seven people in the entire Commission involved in road transport issues and they all sit in adjacent rooms. Each of them is happy to do business with you. We feed them ideas and proposals that help them achieve their stated Commission objectives in this policy domain, which is to reduce road deaths in Europe by 50% by 2010. The Commission drafted this on paper but had no idea how to implement it ... At that time we stepped in and the Commission discovered that it needed the police, and needed the know-how from certain countries.... And things are marching along beautifully now. We are now at the midway point on our timeline and we are right on schedule. And this is about a structural annual reduction in the number of road deaths of no less than 11,000.

TISPOL's director is clearly a man with a mission: to reduce traffic deaths and casualties by beefing up prevention and enforcement on a pan-European scale. Operational necessity got it established, but trust among professionals across borders is what makes it tick. The same goes for all of the other police co-operation networks we studied. With some trust, they can be vibrant, as in the case of Epic described above. But when trust is lacking, as in the Europol case, then progress will remain limited. The following exchange with another senior Dutch police officer highlights this:

Q: *Is there such a thing as a policy framework that dictates whether or not you engage in co-operation with police forces from other countries?*

Yes. It is very simple: do you trust someone or not? It begins with the people involved, and only after that it becomes a matter of organisations or countries.

Q: *What must I do to gain your trust?*

Be open and transparent. You get to know people through international committees and networks. It all starts with interpersonal relationships.

Q: *This trust appears to be very personal. Isn't there some sort of guideline?*

There is a kind of division, for example through Interpol: we do business with so and so, and not with these others – there is a list of this kind. But most of it is individual. You look at the quality of democracy in the other person's country and all that.

Q: What is the ultimate aim for the Dutch police when it comes to international police co-operation?

It would be good if policemen and the mayors and public prosecutors who work with them accept international co-operation as something self-evident. This implies that they should also be convinced that they should devote time to it and be courageous in doing it. It means they will co-operate on the basis of solid agreements and institutionalised trust. Most of all, it is about co-operation becoming something that can be taken for granted.

Street-level entrepreneurs have no intrinsic commitment to the EU project and its main institutions. They try to work through these institutions, but often run up against legal and political constraints. This is especially relevant in the Third Pillar, where the development of EU-wide co-operation is slow and the main advocate for truly post-national policies, the Commission, occupies a weaker position vis-à-vis the member states. Street-level Eurocrats in this domain are constantly confronted by the gap between their felt needs for deeper co-operation and the murky realities of EU practices: they want things for which there are no policies in place yet. Their coping strategy is one of circumvention: bypassing the obstacles of working within the EU institutions by developing alternative forms of co-operation, showing that these do the job, and over time, trying to integrate them into the EU mainstream.

They tend to strive for autonomy, and regard the role of ministries as gatekeepers to participation in relevant EU networks as unhelpful meddling in affairs that could more effectively be settled among professionals. One police chief said:

I don't think that the current government's orientation on putting the citizens first by letting the professionals do their job is properly safeguarded by having us represented in Brussels predominantly by departmental bureaucrats. They are not sufficiently on top of the substance of the issues, which can be quite intricate. It is easy to get it wrong or gloss over the important 'details' if you're not a professional yourself. Besides, it is much easier to build transnational rapport among professionals in a particular field.

They are not comfortable with the world of instructions, mandates, interdepartmental co-ordination, procedural intricacies, forced inclusiveness and logrolling strategies that is part and parcel of the bureaucrat-diplomats' co-operation paradigm.

They instead prefer to build co-operation from the ground up by nurturing personal and professional networks and creating prototypes of practical joint problem-solving that work. One police commissioner put it so eloquently that it is worth quoting him at length:

Since the process of developing European regulations is so extraordinarily time-consuming in the Third Pillar, we at the operational level simply need to create movement in smaller entities. You must, of course, respect state sovereignty and all that, but within these boundaries you must create facts. Take the example of 'joint hitting' in serious crime investigations: we first formed a cross-border team and only asked for The Hague's permission to do so after the fact ... In a way it is all about seduction. Take a concrete shared headache first. You start with sharing information. You start small: concrete and feasible projects. And you take 'safe' forms of co-operation first, such as liaison officers and joint education and training. Then you just happen to organise a conference with your partners from other countries, and then you get the ball rolling ... The trick is to transpose the operational sense of urgency towards the strategic level, the politicians and the very top of the civil service. If at all possible I try to keep the tactical level of middle-level officials out of it, since they tend to be the ones producing all the hurdles. They are more engaged in fighting one another about who gets to head the delegation to the Brussels committees than in facilitating practical co-operation. They are like a thick, impenetrable layer of clay that mutes every movement ... They have another set of roles and responsibilities than we do. They are there to safeguard the uniformity and coherence of Dutch law and policy; we represent the voice of professional service delivery to citizens. And it is a pity that our voice does not get heard directly enough in Brussels. This is why we are lobbying hard to establish a national 'Police House' in Brussels. We number 54,000 policemen and women in this country; if we are not prepared to invest in freeing up some 100 to 150 of them to deal with international co-operation and EU affairs in all their various manifestations, we will simply end up missing the boat.

4.4 Understanding national Eurocrats: Conclusions

In this chapter, we have studied Dutch Eurocrats in the field of European police co-operation in order to understand the worlds they work in, and how
they define and do their work. We suspected that in the relatively open institutional environment of a Third Pillar sector such as police co-operation,
Eurocratic work is less focused on influencing the European Commission
and the drafting of its policy proposals than in a First Pillar sector such as
veterinary policy, as the Commission has little scope for such initiatives under the Third Pillar. So 'getting things done' must entail a different type of
craft, to be practised in different types of arenas. The research reported in
this chapter bears out this expectation. It does, however, yield a varied picture – there is no single, shared notion of 'European policy-making' and 'Eurocratic work' in this sector, there are multiple views which co-exist. Strategic behaviour on the part of member state officials is certainly part of this,
but it takes rather different forms than the tactics described in chapter 3 on
veterinary Eurocrats.

Looking closely at the world of police co-operation, we distilled three
quite distinct logics of Eurocratic work (see table 4.1). In seeking an answer
to our first research question, we found civil servants operating in different
ways in different European arenas. We found bureaucrat-diplomats at the
ministries, as well as in working groups and committees in Brussels, bargaining about national positions. We found street-level entrepreneurs
building transnational coalitions of the willing, as they are confronted with
transnational crime. And we found departmental co-ordinators focused
on making sure the machinery of the domestic preparation of EU policy
processes continues to function smoothly. These are, of course, stylised,
ideal-typical pictures, whereas real-life officials may display these traits to
different degrees and in all sorts of hybrid combinations. But we think the
distinction is useful for analytical and policy purposes.

In part, these different role conceptions simply reflect individual differences, and differences between 'policy bureaucrats' and operational 'doers'. But they are also shaped by the differentiated nature of the European
polity. European governance is produced in bundles of very different types
of policy networks of 'new diplomats', depending on the nature of the col-
laborative challenge at hand (such as exchange, regulation and enforcement; see Slaughter 2004), the institutional context in which joint action
is being shaped (e.g., the position of the issue area in the EU Pillar structure), the level of action involved (policy-making versus operational col-

	Departmental co-ordination bureaucrats	**Bureaucrat-diplomats**	**Street-level entrepreneurs**
Natural habitat	Departmental working groups and interdepartmental meetings of European co-ordinators.	Formal working parties and committees and national preparatory process.	Networks in which information and good practices are exchanged and which strengthen enforcement.
Role orientations	Organising and co-ordinating departmental input and interdepartmental consensus in the preparation of EU meetings. Dominant identity: Dutch civil servant.	Preparing and representing national positions in multilateral forums, and 'selling' the EU in their own home departments. Dominant identity: departmental civil servant.	Operational problem solving. Dominant identity: balancing act between Dutch civil servant and transnational area expert.
Activity and contact patterns	Centred around the roster of (inter)departmental preparatory meetings in anticipation of scheduled EU working group and committee meetings. Consultation with departmental liaison officers at Dutch Permanent Representation.	Centred around scheduled national preparatory meetings and scheduled EU-level working group and committee meetings.	Developing contacts and networks as the need arises and the opportunities for joint action present themselves.
Arenas and channels	Mainly domestic-bureaucratic.	Mainly formal EU forums.	Mainly emergent joint ventures.
Measures of quality and effectiveness	Arriving at agreed-upon, coherent and timely Dutch initiatives and policy positions prior to EU meetings.	Shaping EU agendas and achieving EU policies in accordance with previously agreed-upon Dutch preferences.	Achieving tangible operational successes.
Knowledge and expertise	Knowledge of departmental and interdepartmental EU-related actors and arenas. Knowledge of formal and informal rules of the game in the EU system. Balancing the relative weight and priority of multiple EU dossiers. Ability to capture ministerial and top management attention for participation in EU meetings.	Knowledge of formal and informal rules of the game in the EU system. 'Classic' diplomatic skills (intercultural empathy, language, negotiation, networking etc.). Broad network across the various EU institutions, particularly Commission and EP. Bureau-political skills and clout in the domestic preparatory co-ordination process. Sound grasp of issue substances.	Professional know-how. Broad transborder and/or transnational network in own professional domain. Knowing where to get money and how to overcome potential obstacles in EU system.

Table 4.1 Dutch Eurocrats: three ideal types

laboration), and the need to prepare domestically for positions taken internationally.

Different European action channels pose different demands on national Eurocrats. And so, when compared to the 'old' and deeply institutionalised world of EU veterinary policy as described in chapter 3 or the equally scripted world of the Brussels committee system, there are relatively few precedents and rules to observe for those involved in developing European police co-operation from the ground up. In that arena there is considerable scope for bottom-up agenda-setting and experimentation. There are no fixed allegiances; the challenge is to build coalitions of the willing and find resources to get them going. So, this is part of the answer to the second research question we posed: the way in which European work is organisationally embedded and facilitated is hugely differentiated.

Moreover, co-ordination bureaucrats and bureaucrat-diplomats, on the one hand, and street level-entrepreneurs, on the other, clearly inhabit different worlds. Street level-entrepreneurs complain about departmental co-ordinators and bureaucrat-diplomats knowing too little about 'the real work' (which is about preventing crime and catching criminals in whichever way works); co-ordination bureaucrats and bureaucrat-diplomats complain that street level-entrepreneurs allow tunnel vision and zealotry to disrupt the even-handed development of policy across the full range of dossiers that together constitute the police co-operation portfolio.

Whereas departmental co-ordinators focus on sustaining smooth and timely consultation procedures, bureaucrat-diplomats are preoccupied with articulating and defending the national point of view in multilateral forums, and operational zealots seek to create vehicles for practical transborder co-operation in a truly post-national fashion. The latter's sense of interdependence is strong, simply because the nature of the phenomena they deal with makes it impossible to belie this. Treading cautiously in the formal EU committee settings is not for them, and they seek to work around them. One way to do so is to draw on the ambitions and the financial resources of the European Commission to gain support for smaller-scale 'experiments.' A related way involves building informal 'coalitions of the willing' to find out if and how new forms of co-operation across borders can be made to work, both on the ground and in legal terms. In doing so, they hope to create irreversible facts. The Bureau of Euregional Co-operation in Maastricht described above is one such attempt.

Currently, street-level entrepreneurs rather than bureaucrat-diplomats (or departmental co-ordinators) are the main engines of co-operation and 'integration' in the police co-operation dossier. This may not last. Paradoxically, highly dynamic and successful street-level entrepreneurs, to some extent, sow the seeds of their own demise. As the operational practices they create become more visible and elaborate, pressures to formalise, regulate, and embed them in EU-wide institutional arrangements will grow. To make sure these formalisation processes unfold in desired directions is not something that street-level entrepreneurs are inclined or indeed equipped to do. It will be up to their bureaucratic-diplomatic counterparts to secure and consolidate the fruits of their labour.

Some bureaucrat-diplomats go even further. They are no longer only inclined to produce new rules and regulations, but show a growing awareness that it is part of the problem in police co-operation that for every problem new regulation is decided on. These 'new' bureaucrat-diplomats are aware that to facilitate police co-operation in a way that the police themselves perceive as useful, devising new regulation is not enough. According to them, national departmental officials should co-operate with the police and the European Commission in focusing on practical aspects like facilitating the exchange of information, producing handbooks and who-is-who lists. Perhaps they are representative of a broader phenomenon: national bureaucrat-diplomats who share the typical street-level official's sense of urgency to beef up functional co-operation in areas where it can make a big difference, and in doing so, revitalise the European project. Some street-level bureaucrats have expressed a similar need for these new kinds of ways of co-operation. If their numbers increase, perhaps the various species of Eurocrats discerned in this chapter will blend into a hybrid – the 'complete street-level diplomat'. But for the time being, the day-to-day reality of national administrations seeking to get things done in Europe will continue to involve a delicate balancing act between the different outlooks and operating styles of bureaucrat-diplomats and street-level entrepreneurs.

BRIDGE BUILDERS OR BRIDGEHEADS IN BRUSSELS? THE WORLD OF SECONDED NATIONAL EXPERTS

By Semin Suvarierol and Caspar van den Berg[26]

5.1 Living and breathing the Brussels bureaucracy

The foregoing chapters have demonstrated the extent to which national civil servants are involved in EU-related activities, and the dynamics of national administrative activities in the context of the EU. This chapter shifts the focus from national civil servants working *on* the European Union to national civil servants working *for* the European Union. This is a class of national civil servants for whom finding a balance between national and European interests in their work is a permanent, although sometimes implicit, feature of their daily professional activities. The duality of national and European roles is perhaps the most exacerbated for the seconded national experts (SNEs, see also chapter 3), national civil servants who are temporarily working for EU institutions, in particular those seconded to the European Commission.[27] On the one hand, Commission SNEs have to be loyal to the Commission and represent European interests in this supranational organ of the EU, while on the other hand, their employer remains the member state government, and they are thus expected to return to their home organisation after their secondment term ends. Therefore, the SNEs are practically torn between two employers: their daily employer under whose supervision they work (the Commission) and the national employer who sent them on the secondment and continues to pay their salaries (the member state).

Besides these atypical terms of employment, SNEs also form a particular group of European civil servants in terms of their position at a crossing point of European and national governance at the micro level. This key position stems mainly from their presence in the beginning phase of the EU legislative process by working for the Commission. As has been argued in chapter 3, SNEs are potentially key strategic instruments for the member states in manoeuvring policy proposals. Conversely, SNEs are key resources for the Commission to sound out the acceptability of a particular proposal for a given member state. This reciprocal gain, however, can only work if there is an ongoing flow of information between the Commission and the member state through the SNE. By virtue of the flow of information, SNEs can play a major role in linking the European and the national level through their *networks* or 'know-who' at both levels. To the extent that these networks are maintained, both the Commission and the member state can benefit optimally from the 'know-how' of SNEs. Furthermore, since networks are attached to people, they can remain intact when the secondment ends, which can make the benefits of the secondment period long-lasting. The lasting benefits can only be reaped, however, if SNEs return to their home organisation and keep on working *on* Europe in positions where they can make use of their networks.

Based on this premise, this chapter asks how the work of SNEs can be characterised as connectors between the national and European administration: they utilise their networks, rather as *bridge builders* between the Commission and the member state, or do they primarily act as national *bridgeheads* in the supranational Commission arena? Answers to a number of sub-questions are necessary to arrive at this insight:

- To what extent do the SNEs rely on their national networks during their secondment?
- For what purposes do they use their networks?
- Do these networks endure? In other words, to what extent do the SNEs rely on their European network upon their return?
- To what extent does the Dutch government exert substantive influence through its SNEs (by means of signalling and frontloading)?
- To what extent is a period of secondment with the European Commission a route for career advancement for Dutch civil servants?

The remainder of this chapter is organised as follows: First, the methodology and empirical data are presented. A short discussion of the secondment system will be followed by some remarks concerning the particularities of the Netherlands as a supplier of SNEs. We will review the answers to our questions and make conclusions by reflecting on the implications of our findings for the effective use of SNEs as a strategic tool (as implied in chapter 3).

5.2 Getting inside the insiders: Methodology and data

Empirical research focusing on seconded national experts is rare. The growing significance of SNEs within the Commission has only recently received attention in the literature, namely through the work of Jarle Trondal (2004, 2006a, 2006b). Trondal was the first scholar to collect data on SNEs. The sample of respondents he uses in his work includes mainly Swedish and Norwegian SNEs, and his work analyses the identities and allegiances of these officials. We chose to concentrate on national experts from one member state and arrive at valid results for this specific group. This also allowed us to explore to what extent SNEs fulfil their dual role of carrying expertise from the member state to the Commission and from the Commission back to the member state.

The Netherlands presents an interesting case in this regard. Not only did it long enjoy a reputation as an enthusiastic subscriber to the ideal of an integrated Europe, but as one of the founding members of the European Union it is a longstanding player in the secondment system. Secondly, its modest size makes it possible for researchers to identify and reach the entire population of current SNEs and a considerable share of the population of former SNEs for the period between 2001 and 2005 (56%) with relative ease. Our dataset is composed of 90 Dutch national experts divided into two groups: one group of officials who are currently working as SNEs at the European Commission and one group of former SNEs who were seconded between 2001 and 2005.[28] For both groups of respondents, we collected survey and interview data. The survey and interview questions have been adapted from Trondal's SNE studies to Dutch SNEs. The aim of the survey has been to obtain an overview on the networks, positions and careers of a large group of SNEs so as to follow up with in-depth interviews with a smaller group of SNEs on the major aspects that came to the fore through the surveys.

The entire population of the current 62 Dutch SNEs was contacted to participate in the survey,[29] out of which 46 responded to our request, resulting in a 74% response rate. Hence we can be confident that our data for the current Dutch SNEs are representative (Babbie 1992 267). In-depth interviews were conducted with eight of these officials, selected on the basis of the range of responses they gave, with the aim of covering the broadest range with a small number of respondents.

The former SNEs were reached using the snowballing method due to the absence of complete records. Out of a population of 91 former SNEs, we were able to contact 51,[30] and 44 of the contacted former SNEs filled in the questionnaire (a response rate of 86%). The use of snowball rather than random sampling does not pose great problems for interpreting the results, since we only report frequencies, means and medians in our analysis. In addition, 20 in-depth interviews have been conducted with this group of respondents. The item non-response rate was low for the surveys, the poorest item score was 78 respondents. The survey questions have been streamlined to enable comparison between the two groups of SNEs. The former SNEs have been asked questions regarding their secondment period and their current functions to enable cross-time comparisons.[31]

5.3 Demand and supply: The Dutch and the expert secondment system

The growing number of tasks accorded to the European level of governance over the years has brought up the need for more staff, which has led the European Commission to increasingly resort to external assistance through temporary employment arrangements, partly due to budgetary stringency and partly to changing agendas that require extra expertise. There are 22,543 officials working for the Commission, 6,868 of whom are external or temporary staff.[32] Seconded national experts number 1,077, but their relative weight is better understood when one takes into consideration that their number equals 9.7% of the total number of 11,052 policy officials (Administrator/A-level officials), i.e., the highest level of Commission officials.

The primary aim of the secondment system is to inject into the Commission the high level of professional knowledge in a specific area of expertise and work experience in the member state the national experts possess, especially in areas where such expertise is lacking within the Commission's rank and file. The potential benefit for the national administrations in return is that SNEs increase their expertise at the European/international level while gaining insider knowledge on the institutional set-up and functioning of the EU, which, one presumes, they take back to their administrations.

SNEs are typically seconded from the administrations (national, regional or local) of EU member states, though the Commission also recruits experts from the private and voluntary sectors or international organisations where their expertise is needed. SNE vacancies are usually made public by informing the Permanent Representations of member states in Brussels, which subsequently contact the respective national authorities. The recruiting Commission unit receives the applications of SNE candidates from the member states, makes a shortlist and selects an SNE, usually as a result of an interview. The secondment lasts between six months and four years during which the SNE is remunerated by their home employer and receives compensation from the Commission for the extra costs incurred by living and working abroad.[33] Whereas it is a relatively cheap matter to hire experts for the Commission, Dutch government organisations, for instance, invest an estimated total of three million euros annually through continued salaries on seconded officials.[34]

From the outset, SNEs have a double allegiance: they are employees of their home organisation (financially and officially), but they work under the instructions of the European Commission. SNEs are obliged to behave solely in the interests of the Commission and not to accept any instructions or duties from their home government or organisation. But they do not have the authority to represent the Commission or to enter into any commitments on behalf of the Commission.[35] This double role is further exacerbated by the fact that the entire secondment system is based on the assumption that SNEs return to their home organisation after the termination of their secondment. SNEs cannot escape the permanent balancing act this arrangement entails. As one interviewee stated: 'The Commission is my boss, but I will return, so I do take Dutch interests into consideration. For instance, I am careful with my criticisms of the Netherlands. On the other hand, the more you sound like a representative of the Netherlands, the less authority you wield in the Commission. So you have to be objective.'[36]

The Commission is organised primarily according to sector and function, which makes it structurally comparable to a national administration. What differentiates the Commission is its multinational staff. In order to prevent any particular nationalities from dominating the ranks of the Commission, the organisation has from the beginning respected a 'geographical balance' rule whereby the number of staff employed by the Commission reflects approximately the population size to ensure a legitimate composition. Dutch officials currently make up 3.3% of the total and 4% of A-level officials of the Commission. The Netherlands comprises 3.6% of the EU population and 4% of the weighted Council votes. Thus, the Dutch share of Commission officials is largely in proportion to its geographical entitlement. Until recently, however, the Netherlands was under-represented within the Commission bureaucracy. This under-representation partially stemmed from the fact that the entrance exam for permanent officials, the *concours*, was difficult to pass for Dutch candidates because competitive examinations are fairly unknown in the Dutch educational system. This led

POLICY AREA	DIRECTORATE-GENERAL	FREQUENCY	PERCENT
	DG Competition	9	
Market-oriented	DG Internal Market and	7	
	Services	4	
	DG Economic and Financial Affairs	4	
	DG Enterprise		
	Total	*24*	*26.7%*
	DG Environment	7	
	DG Health and Consumer		
Social	Protection	5	
Regulation	DG Employment	4	
	DG Justice	4	
	DG Education and Culture	1	
	Total	*21*	*23.3%*
	DG Transport and Energy	7	
	DG Research	5	
	DG Taxation and Customs		
Supply side	Union	4	
	DG Information Society and Media	3	
	Total	*19*	*21.1%*
	Eurostat	4	
	DG Budget	2	
	Secretariat-General	2	
Administration	Legal Service	2	
	OLAF (European Anti-Fraud Office)	1	
	Total	*11*	*12.2%*
	DG External Relations	3	
External affairs	DG Trade	3	
	DG Enlargement	2	
	Total	*8*	*8.9%*
	DG Agriculture	5	
Provision	DG Development	2	
	Total	*7*	*7.8%*
		N= 90	100%

Table 5.1 Commission Directorate-Generals as SNE Receivers

the Dutch government to take active measures aimed at increasing the number of Dutch officials, e.g., by introducing training courses for the *concours* and appointing an official to the Dutch EU Permanent Representation responsible for co-ordinating Dutch appointments to EU institutions.[37]

Secondments, meanwhile, have been a safe way to secure Dutch posts. Furthermore, the secondment system allows the country to send the 'right people' to Brussels and to create a good image so that the Commission actually requests Dutch SNEs.[38] The Dutch SNE policy seems to have reached this target since the Netherlands is currently the home of 62 SNEs to the European Commission, which comprises 5.8% of the SNE population. This, however, is not exclusively due to government strategy. There are two other factors that help to explain the relative over-representation of Dutch officials among SNEs. One is the proximity of the Netherlands to Belgium, which makes it possible to keep one foot in the home country during the secondment. The personal lives of potential Dutch SNEs suffer less than those of their colleagues from further afield.[39] Secondly and perhaps more importantly, is the fact that the Netherlands has a high level of expertise in the fields sought by the Commission, such as transport, research, environment, agriculture and financial markets.[40] Table 5.1 indicates the distribution of respondent SNEs across policy areas and Commission DGs.

The table shows that half of the respondents were deployed within either the market-oriented or the social regulation DGs, and that the top four receiving DGs were DG Competition, DG Internal Market and Service, DG Environment and DG Transport and Energy.

Looking at the ministries and agencies that provide SNEs, the percentages by policy area are somewhat different than the percentages per policy area for the receiving DGs. These differences are accounted for by the differences in organisational arrangements between the EU and Dutch central administration level.

POLICY AREA	MINISTRY	FREQUENCY	PERCENT
Market-oriented	FIN (Ministry of Finance)	13	
	EZ (Ministry of Economic Affairs)	9	
	NMA (Competition Authority)	3	
	DNB (National Reserve Bank)	3	
	AFM (Financial Markets Authority)	1	
	OPTA (Telecom Authority)	1	
	Total	*29*	*33%*
Provision	LNV (Ministry of Agriculture)	14	
	Productschap Akkerbouw (Arable Farming Commodity Board)	2	
	Total	*16*	*18%*
Social Regulation	SoZaWe (Ministry of Social Affairs)	5	
	MinJus (Ministry of Justice)	4	
	VROM (Ministry of Housing, Spatial Planning and Environment)	3	
	VWS (Ministry of Health)	1	
	BVE Raad (Educational Board)	1	
	OCW (Ministry of Education)	1	
	Total	*16*	*18%*
Supply side	VandW (Ministry of Transport)	9	
	Senter (Office for Sustainability and Innovation)	1	
	Syntens (Entrepreneurial Innovation Office)	1	
	Agentschap Douane (Customs Office)	1	
	TNO (Institute for Applied Sciences)	1	
	FOM (Foundation for Fundamental Research on Matter)	1	
	European Science Foundation	1	
	Total	*15*	*17%*
External affairs	BuZa (Ministry of Foreign Affairs)	9	10%
Administration	CBS (Statistical Bureau)	3	
	CPB (Bureau for Economic Policy Analysis)	1	
	Total	*4*	*4%*
		N= 89	100%

Table 5.2 Dutch ministries and agencies as SNE Providers

Not surprisingly, the top five suppliers of SNEs are the Ministry of Agriculture, Nature and Food Safety, the Ministry of Finance (including the Dutch Tax and Customs Administration), the Ministry of Economic Affairs, the Ministry of Transport, Public Works and Water Management and the Ministry of Foreign Affairs.

There is a clear parallel between the organisations that are key providers of SNEs and the organisations with the highest density of Europeanised civil servants (chapter 2). Four out of the top five suppliers of SNEs feature in the cluster of 'Eurocratic bulwarks', the Ministry of Finance and the Tax Administration being the only exceptions as Eurocratic runners-up. This can be seen as strengthening the validity of the 'league table of EU-ness' of Dutch public organisations presented in chapter 2.

5.4 Profiling the Dutch expert contingent

Who are the Dutch SNEs? Based on our survey and interview data, we construct a profile of Dutch SNEs with respect to their education level, age and rank prior to secondment, and type of home organisation.

Based on the nature of the activities of SNE positions and on the interview responses, we infer that all SNEs are highly educated (HBO-level and up) and that the overwhelming majority holds a university degree (Bachelors/Masters/PhD). Of the total group of respondents, 38% started their secondment between the ages of 25 and 34, 33% between the ages of 35 and 44, 21% between 45 and 54, and 8% over 55. The average age at the start of secondment was 40. This indicates that the Dutch government seconds predominantly young to middle-age officials who are presumably at the beginning or in the middle of their careers. With respect to the rank of an SNE upon secondment, some interesting patterns can be observed, as shown in table 5.3.

About 63% of the SNEs were in ranks 10 to 12 prior to the start of their secondment, 31% were in ranks 13 and 14, and 6% were in ranks 15 and 16. The average prior rank among the total group of SNEs was 12.47. These figures seem to underline the assertion that EU-level activity among national civil servants is more the domain of middle-level civil servants than of top-ranking civil servants, (Noordegraaf 2000; 't Hart et al. 2002). The trend that the frequency of SNEs decreases as rank increases is largely explained by the fact that SNE positions are mostly policy-making posts, and policy preparation becomes increasingly less common as a main activity for civil servants

	FORMER SNEs	CURRENT SNEs	TOTAL
Higher civil servants (Ranks: 10-12)	28 (66.7%)	24 (58.5%)	52 (62.7%)
Senior civil servants (Ranks: 13-14)	14 (33.3%)	12 (29.3%)	26 (31.3%)
Top civil servants (Ranks: 15-16)	0 (0%)	5 (12.2%)	5 (6.0%)
TOTAL	42 (100%)	41 (100%)	N=83 (100%)

Table 5.3 Ranks of Dutch SNEs at the time of secondment

in ranks 14 and above.[43] In section 5.6, we will return to the issue of rank, within the framework of the discussion on career development through the secondment system.

In the previous section, we already indicated the distribution of SNEs in terms of their home organisations (table 5.1). Introducing the dichotomy of executive agency vs. policy department (see also chapter 2), we observe that 76% of all respondents originated from policy departments, and 24% from executive agencies. Apart from the fact that part of this difference is explained by the fact that most SNE positions are policy positions and many fewer are executive positions, assuming that the share of SNEs delivered by each type of organisation is a valid indicator of EU involvement, our findings are analogous with the conclusion found in chapter 2.3.2, namely that policy departments are more involved in EU affairs than executive agencies.

With respect to the duration of the secondment, we observe that 17% of the SNEs were seconded for less than a year, 34% for a period between one and two years, 30% between two and three years, and 19% between three and four years.[44] So, the large majority of SNEs remains at the Commission for about two years. A two-year stay is bound to provide enough time to supply substantive contributions to the work in the Commission and to constitute a substantial improvement for the individual SNE in terms of skills and knowledge on the EU. If we consider the fact that 49% of Dutch SNEs stay in the Commission between two to four years, this period of time is presumably also long enough to build a network at the EU, if not at the transnational level. Does the secondment period translate into returns for the SNEs and the Dutch government in terms of networks and knowledge and can the Dutch SNEs exchange their value-added for better career opportunities which involve them using this EU know-who and know-how?

5.5 Knowing how and knowing who: Networking

We borrow our definitions of transnational policy networks from the multi-level governance literature where the role of informal bargaining between a very wide variety of actors (individuals and institutions, public and private, local, regional, national, European, international) is suggested to be at least as decisive as formal power relations. *Policy networks* are defined here as 'more or less stable sets of public and private organisational actors, linked to each other by communication and by the exchange of resources, such as information and expertise' (Jönsson et al. 1998: 326). They consist of the contacts, ties and connections between actors that develop as a complement to formal institutional relations. The emergence of these networks is conditional upon the development of personal relations between relevant actors, which in turn depends on their frequency of interaction. As such, policy networks bring together individuals originating from different fields of knowledge and social environments.

The significance of policy networks within EU governance is twofold: '*know-how*' and '*know-who*', i.e., an actor needs to have thorough substantive knowledge, as well as knowledge of the organisations, procedures, and individuals who shape the policy environment (Jönsson and Strömvik 2005: 18). Furthermore, these networks are *transnational* and involve both governmental and non-governmental policy actors. Experts may be linked with one another by means of vertical (i.e., across levels of governance), horizontal (i.e., across policy sectors and/or across government, corporate and research organisations) and potentially also diagonal (i.e., cutting through both vertical and horizontal orderings) relations (Slaughter 2004, see also chapter 1). These multilateral network links allow bureaucrats at various levels of governance to prepare and implement policies assisted by organised interests supplying technically relevant expertise. This is the essence of network governance (Kohler-Koch and Eising 1999).

To investigate to what extent SNEs form a bridge between their own member state and the European Commission, we asked both groups of SNEs questions involving the frequency of their reliance on their network in the Netherlands and the Commission. A majority of current Dutch SNEs

(53.3%) reported drawing upon the network they built in the Netherlands prior to their secondment once a week. Another 47.7% said they were approached monthly by their former colleagues at the Dutch organisation they worked for. Only 18.2% of the former SNEs were approached weekly and 34.1% monthly by their former colleagues during their secondment period. Clearly, the current Dutch SNEs have more frequent contacts with their network in the Netherlands. Their contacts also involve sending written information to their home organisation – 53.3% have such contacts monthly.

What does this network entail, however? To what extent do SNEs build up and become part of transnational networks extending to different administrative levels in different member states, to non-state players, and other EU and international organisations? Or are they just individual bridges between the Commission and the member state they come from? And, since policy networks are assumed to be relatively stable and persistent; what happens to these networks after the secondment period? To what extent do the bridges remain intact?

Who's in the loop?

We will first look at the frequency of SNE contacts across different levels and actors. Since the scale employed does not have equal intervals, we use the median to compare the results.

Survey Questions:
- **Current SNEs:** How frequently do you have work-related contacts and/or meetings with the following during your secondment?
- **Former SNEs:** How frequently did you have work-related contacts and/or meetings with the following during your secondment? / How frequently do you have work-related contacts and/or meetings with the following in your current function?

Answer categories: Once per day=5, Once per week=4, Once per month=3, Once per year=2, Never=1

	Median: Current SNEs	Median: Former SNEs during secondment	Median: Former SNEs in current function
Colleagues within other DGs	4	4	
SNEs from:			
- The Netherlands	3	3	3
- Other member states	4	4	
Other EU institutions	3	3	2
Other international organisations	3	3	2
The Dutch EU Permanent Representation	3	3	1
EU Permanent Representations of other member states	2	2	1
Dutch national administration:			
- Own policy sector	4	3	4
- Other policy sectors	2	2	3
National administrations of other member states:			
- Own policy sector	3	3	2
- Other policy sectors	1	1	1
Representatives of regional governments from:			
- The Netherlands	1	1	1
- Other member states	1	1	1
Representatives of local governments from:			
- The Netherlands	1	1	1
- Other member states	1	1	1
Representatives of the private sector from:			
- The Netherlands	3	3	3
- Other member states	2.5	2	1
Representatives of NGOs from:			
- The Netherlands	1	2	1
- Other member states	1	2	1
Universities or research institutes from:			
- The Netherlands	2	2	2
- Other member states	2	2	1

Table 5.4 Frequency of Dutch SNE contacts

If we concentrate on the medians higher than 2, since this offers the most regular contacts, we see that only a few actors actually fall into this category. The most frequent contacts are within the Commission and with the Dutch national administration within the officials' own policy sector. Other EU institutions, international organisations, the Dutch EU Permanent Representation, and sectoral contacts with other member states are the most forthcoming contact points in the supranational and national arena. The non-governmental aspect among the SNE networks is occupied by Dutch, and to a lesser extent, by European business.

The figures for the contacts of past SNEs during their secondment follow a similar pattern with few exceptions.[47] When we turn to the network patterns of former SNEs in their current function, however, we see that their contacts are clustered predominantly within the Dutch national administration. Meanwhile, the Commission and Dutch business figures are the other most forthcoming network partners. The results clearly show that the only lasting transnational or supranational networks for SNEs are within the Commission.

A number of conclusions can be drawn from these observations. The SNE secondment system does stimulate the formation of transnational networks, but applying these data to the three types of network relations set out in this article, we see that the network connections fall largely under the vertical dimension of network relations, to a lesser degree under the horizontal dimension, and only to a very limited extent under the diagonal dimension of network relations. Therefore, the SNEs do indeed form bridges between the Commission and the member state and provide a channel for the flow of information, ideas and contacts.

Networking as strategic behaviour

How do the SNEs fulfil this bridging function in practice? Of the three avenues for strategic behaviour available to member-state governments, signalling, frontloading and the coalition-building introduced in chapter 3, SNEs play a significant role in the first two. SNEs, especially in the pre-proposal stage, can use their position within the Commission and the wider networks to influence the content of proposals.[48] As one SNE emphasised, 'Apart from the SNEs, The Hague has no access whatsoever to what happens in the early stages of the Commission's legislative process.'[49]

SNEs facilitate signalling in the sense that they offer easy access points for national civil servants and officials at the Permanent Representation so that they can pursue certain national interests or concerns within the Commission apparatus and vice versa. When Dutch government officials begin seeking an access point within the Commission, they first seek out a fellow-national to talk to.[50] This usually means an SNE, who plays the role of a switchboard within the Commission. Roughly half of former SNEs and the majority of the current SNEs (63% of the interview respondents) indicate they were relatively frequently used as an 'EU helpdesk' for the members of their home organisations. Words they use to describe their role include: 'feeler', 'resonance box', 'ambassador', 'antenna', 'brainstorming partner' but also 'missionary' and 'infiltrator'.

The practice of signalling rests on trust-based reciprocity, and the necessary level of trust can stem from nationality or previous trust-generating interactions. In this sense, the SNE networks make the flow of information between the Commission and the member state possible:

> I have personal contacts with my former colleagues. My Ministry approaches me first. I discuss the issues with colleagues who call. The other way around, when there is a new strategy I will first sound out ideas with colleagues in the Netherlands in order to use existent knowledge in the Netherlands within the ministries.[51]

Signalling can thus work in two directions:

> Your SNE position makes it possible to notify colleagues at home, so that they can anticipate the Commission's course of action. For instance, they can prepare sabotage strategies, proposals for amendment or forge alliances. In some cases, the timing of a member state entering the policy game is decided by the SNE.[52]

In terms of the Commission, both the network and the experience of the SNE at the national level are valuable for the Commission because:

> ... the permanent officials do not need to have any experience or network at the national administration level. This is the value-added of an SNE. At the end of the day, the Commission focuses on member states, so it is important to have a network within these member states. Furthermore, the officials have no experience with practice. As an SNE, you learn a lot about what happens on the ground in practice. That is a big asset. You just know how it works and how things are implemented.[53]

It is in the Commission's interest to know what the member state is considering.[54] In turn, the information is then channelled to the Commission which can thus be used as input on a proposal.

The importance of SNEs with respect to frontloading, is even more crucial, given that the appointment of SNEs within a specific DG is the central instrument for this type of strategic behaviour. That the Dutch Ministry of Agriculture, among others, sends its officials to strategic positions in the Commission, as argued in chapter 3, finds support in the account of an SNE seconded from this ministry:

> Your influence depends on your position. I work in the field of phytosanitary and veterinary trade barriers. Of course, the Netherlands has a strategic interest in this area. It is interesting to see how the Commission deals with this issue. As an exporting country, it is very important to have someone at such a strategic position within the Commission, both for the Netherlands and for my own Ministry.[55]

In short: strategic appointments in view of certain important dossiers are a pivotal method of frontloading.

The other two mechanisms through which frontloading is secured as a strategic route are (a) through instructions from superior; and (b) as a result of the national-cultural perspective taken by the SNE in question on the policy issue. Dutch SNEs claim that they do not receive any direct instructions from the Dutch government, which is quite different from SNEs of other member states:

> There are countries with an SNE policy. The UK sends instructions and influences opinion-building with position papers. The French SNEs are also given follow-ups. The Netherlands does this less. You sometimes end up reading the national position bij chance in a newsletter.[56]

While some SNEs believe they should exert national influence, others believe the influence should be exercised by the Dutch Permanent Representation instead.[57] In that sense, some SNEs seem to totally endorse their Commission identity: 'Expertise is the most important. We are not the member state representatives here. They are in the Council.'[58]

Still, the secondment system offers the member state the opportunity to support EU files with its own people.[59] This happens via the direct involvement of SNEs in the Commission. They can 'make the Dutch voice heard in Brussels.'[60] This is actually what our Dutch SNE respondents consider the frontloading method, which is much more common and much more appropriate in terms of exercising influence. The Ministry does not need to dictate to SNEs since they already have an indirect influence over them by way of the process of 'thinking as a Dutchman'.[61] This is also a transparent national method, since the proposal drafted by a Dutch SNE still needs to pass through all the official EU procedures. Thus, this viewpoint gets locked into the proposal and might be altered at various junctures, but the general spirit rarely changes substantially. In other words, the first blow is half the battle, and SNEs play a pivotal role in enabling member-states to strike that first blow.

With respect to the contribution to the policy process, the nationality of an SNE influences his or her way of thinking:[62] 'Although you never have a substantial mandate, what you do bring to the table in the policy-making process is a Dutch point of view on the policy issue in question.'[63] As another SNE observed:

> The SNE brings his own experience, way of thinking, and problem-solving strategy to the Commission, all of which have been developed within a specific framework of one's home country. Once you are faced with real policy issues at the Commission, the first reflex is to fall back into one's old routines. As time goes by, he may place issues within a wider, more European framework, but still the SNE's prior experience – or even the tradition he comes from – continues to play a large role.[64]

Furthermore, many SNEs reported that while they were seconded they continued to follow the Dutch media (newspapers, television, etc.) and that for a considerable part, their social lives remained more centred in the Netherlands than in Brussels. As a result of the stronger links that SNEs have with their home countries compared to permanent Commission officials, SNEs are also better able to reflect the stakes of a member state and to anticipate national policy positions.[65] An interesting distinction that both current and former SNEs made is the one between Dutch permanent Commission officials and SNEs. Permanent Dutch officials have reportedly far less direct contact with officials at the national administration level than SNEs. At the same time, SNEs perceive permanent officials as being more independent in relation to their member's home country. This seems to indicate that the width and depth of an official's network in the member state does not depend so much on an official's nationality, but more on whether the official is pre-socialised in a national context and whether the official is legally bound to the national administration.

One SNE noted that the national perspective taken by the SNE serves the benefit of the Commission, too:

> It is very common to present the problems or positions of your member-state. I was also regularly approached by other Commission civil servants who wanted to put out their feelers in the early stages to find out whether or not a specific proposal would be greeted with enthusiasm by the Netherlands. So, the presence of SNEs allows for a smoother and quicker policy process because SNEs are normally well aware of various national positions.[66]

However, it should be noted that the mere presence of SNEs within the various DGs does not automatically lead to a successful outcome and that the degree of success is contingent upon the degree of co-ordination of SNE activity from the national department and the effectiveness of the SNE in mobilising his or her network to influence the authors of a policy proposal. This leads to the situation where member states have the opportunity to have an impact on the policy-making process if they can second their civil servants purposefully and strategically. The Dutch government seems to have adopted this strategic approach with the aim of gaining more access to the EU by building and sharing experiences through the secondment system.[67]

However, roughly half of the former SNEs reported that there was not enough interest on the part of their seconding organisation for the potential gains that secondment could have for these organisations. 'Out of sight, out of mind', was a very frequent description of the perceived attitude of the sending organisation towards the SNE during the secondment. Many pointed out that it was they who had to take the initiative of contacting their home ministry, and that the ministry did not make enough use of their presence in the Commission. The situation may be changing, however: our data signals a difference between the current and the former SNEs in terms of the degree of contact between the home organisation and the SNE during secondment (see table 5.4). It seems that the contacts between SNEs and their home organisations have indeed increased over the past few years. A second conceivable explanation for this variation is the potential propensity by officials to think more positively about 'the relationship with their home organisation during their secondment' *while* they are seconded rather than *after* their return, given that many respondents were disappointed by the treatment they received from their home organisations upon return, which seems to be common as the following sections suggest.

Do SNE networks persist?

The empirical evidence above demonstrates the bridging function of seconded officials *during* their secondment. However, the lasting effects of the secondment system can only be assessed by addressing the question of whether the bridge remains intact after the secondment. Using the knowledge and networks they acquired during the secondment is the most crucial payoff of the secondment system for the member state government: 'When you know the internal procedures of the EU, you can anticipate instead of reacting. Your Commission network allows to keep on anticipating. This is perhaps more important than anything else. The ministries, in turn, acquire more of an understanding of what can be done and what cannot.'[68]

Several respondents observed that building up and maintaining a network with people at the Commission level is easier than maintaining a network with officials at the national level. The organisational culture at the Commission level is apparently more open to establishing longer-term professional and social contacts than the organisational culture in their Dutch home organisations.[69] Since not all SNEs originate from within the Dutch central government, but also from agencies and semi-governmental institutions, the secondment system can also help create networks between the SNE and governmental actors at the national level, which may become beneficial once the secondment has ended.

Our findings convincingly show, however, that although the expertise of Dutch ministries/authorities flows largely toward the Commission, the Dutch administration does not always get the EU expertise back. In other words, the bridge is often one-way: only 27 of 43 (62.8%) former SNEs from our sample still work for the organisation they worked for prior to their secondment.[70]

This means that network ties in turn also seem to grow weaker once an SNE returns – 27.5% of the former SNEs stated that they continue to use the network they established during their secondment in their current function at least once a month while another 25% use it only once a year, and 17.5% do not use their Commission network at all.

It is also striking that current SNEs expressed relatively high hopes regarding the degree to which they believe they will be able to professionally utilise their networks, while the majority of former SNEs demonstrated their disappointment with respect to how much they actually use their networks in their present jobs since their secondment. Given that many former SNEs also reported that they had considerable expectations in this respect before and during their secondment, we interpret these differences as an indication of overly optimistic prospects on the part of current SNEs rather than an increase in the levels of opportunities to utilise acquired networks upon their return to their home administrations.

During the interviews with former SNEs, many respondents indicated that their networks within and, when applicable, outside the Commission had grown outdated and were thus of little or no use. This is remarkable, considering that the secondments of our respondents had ended on average only two years earlier. In most cases, the reason for their networks becoming outdated was the fact that their first job after the secondment did not require their networks. A considerable number of these respondents noted that while they made little to no use of their established networks professionally, they did maintain personal contacts with their secondment colleagues.

Some of these respondents, with current jobs that do not enable them to make formal professional use of their networks, did indicate that the personal contacts they maintained did yield some information, which may or may not have a bearing on their current employment, although some of it was sometimes of interest to their organisations. They were convinced that their present colleagues for whom this information might be relevant did not get the same information as timely: 'Through my network at the Commission I get information about issues that no one else within my organisation has access to;'[71] and 'It is always nice to have more information on an issue or receive it earlier than your boss, for instance. Because I know a number of people at the Commission, I get this informational advantage vis-à-vis my boss.'[72] These respondents reported networks form a more personal and indirect way back into their organisations.

Others who felt their network had, to some extent, dissolved indicated that a large part of their network had already left Brussels as well, and that they did not have new contact information for most of these people. Nevertheless, respondents who indicated that their networks were outdated did acknowledge that their secondments and their familiarity with the structures of the Commission gave them an advantage in building up new networks in their current jobs.

On the contrary, former SNEs with jobs that still have a good connection at the Commission reported that the benefits of their acquired networks were substantial. This indicates a positive correlation between, on the one hand, the degree of compatibility between the jobs SNEs had during secondment and the jobs they now held, and, on the other hand, the degree to which officials have been able to maintain their networks and utilise them professionally.

5.6 Life after secondment: SNEs and their careers

If the Dutch government wants the benefits of its investments in the SNEs not only during but *after* their secondment, there needs to be a proactive career planning programme for the SNEs upon their return. The reality, however, has been quite different. First, since only 62.8% of SNEs actually return, it is clear that the current 'return guarantee' is insufficient to ensure any return on investment.

SNE interviewees have pointed out the gap between expectations built up in Brussels and the reality upon their return to The Hague. The high expectations stem from the fact that SNEs feel they grow enormously during their secondments and expect to be rewarded for this upon their return. The reality is often quite different, so much so that current SNEs tend to be concerned about their futures based on their knowledge of their predecessors' fates:

> The return policy is an important issue. SNEs gain substantial and practical knowledge at the EU institutions. There is currently is no management system in place to take care of what happens after secondment. Secondment is not a promotion. Until now, SNEs have not been rewarded upon return. Some have been promoted away. Now that the number of SNEs has doubled, it is time to overhaul the policies concerning returning SNEs. After all, secondment should be good for your career.[73]

However, when looking at their national careers upon their return, we see that secondment entails stagnation, since SNEs maintain the same rank during the entire secondment period regardless of their personal growth. They return to the same job and rank, which constitutes a relative loss of opportunity for many who would have otherwise had a chance for promotion.[74] At the same time, their peers at the ministry in The Hague continue to rise among the ranks, as they are still visible to their superiors at the ministry whereas the SNE in Brussels also becomes also 'out of sight and out of mind' in terms of their career planning. In the words of an SNE: 'In the Netherlands, they are not sitting and waiting for you. They say: "Are you still alive? We have to find something for you." So it is not good for your career in the Netherlands.'[75]

The fears of the current SNEs find life in the experience of former SNEs. One observation seems to represent the sentiments of a large number of former SNE's:

> Beforehand I expected that the secondment would offer me additional career opportunities, but as it turned out, this was by no means the case. For those who managed to get a permanent position with the Commission afterwards, it has obviously paid off. But all the people I know that have been seconded are disappointed in terms of the supposed advantage that they were to get out of their secondment. No wonder that most of them leave within a year after they have returned to work elsewhere where their Brussels experience does get valued.[76]

Former SNEs were asked whether they believed that their secondment had offered them any career advancement, 51% answered negatively.[77]

Comparing the present ranks of former SNEs with the ranks they had just before being seconded, it turns out that among those who were seconded in the period 2000-2005, 57% were still at the same rank, 29% had moved up one rank, while 11% had moved up two ranks (the remaining 3% represents one individual who had actually been demoted one rank). In other words, of the former SNEs included in our study, 60% had not been significantly promoted, during or since the completion of their secondment. The average upward mobility among this group during an average period of 3.75 years was by 0.49 in rank. Although we have not been able to compare this figure with national civil servants of the same age, educational level and organisation during the same period, this rate of upward mobility is by no means spectacular.

As long as this image is sustained and there is no concrete career planning, the SNEs will continue to take steps in their career that ultimately decrease their chance of returning to their original ministry employers. Their old positions do not offer enough challenges, which urges many to begin searching for alternative employment, whether it is in Brussels or in the private sector in the Netherlands.

CURRENT SECTOR	RETURN to PREVIOUS ORGANISATION		Frequency (Percent)
	Yes	No	
Public	25	4	29 (67.4%)
Semi-public	2	3	5 (11.6%)
Private	0	4	4 (9.3%)
Public international (Commission, IO)	0	3	3 (7.0%)
None (Retired)	0	2	2 (4.7%)
TOTAL	27 (62.8%)	16 (27.2%)	N=43

Table 5.5 SNE return rate after secondment

As the figures for the former SNEs show, SNEs who do not return to their home organisation make career moves in various directions.

One remarkable exception here is the Ministry of Agriculture SNEs. This 'Eurocratic bulwark' ministry in particular scores very high in terms of luring its SNEs back: of the eight Agriculture SNEs, seven of them are still working for the ministry. This is because, interviewees pointed out, the Ministry of Agriculture has a more consistent policy regarding their SNEs. While some did end up in their old positions, others obtained promotions to positions that matched their profiles.[78] Thus the Ministry's reputation as a true 'Eurocratic bulwark' (see chapter 2) also applies to its career management of its SNEs.

On the whole, however, a secondment with the Commission can hardly be seen as a route to career advancement for those involved. Being seconded has actually had a negative career effect, at least for some of the SNEs who were seconded in the early years of the 21st century. This is not a typical Dutch phenomenon. A survey among former SNEs from various member states conducted in 2002 shows that problems regarding career advancement were a general phenomenon associated with the entire secondment system.[79]

5.7 An under-utilised asset: Conclusions

Our empirical data on Dutch former and current SNEs show that SNEs do build bridges between the EU and the member state via their roles in forming and sometimes maintaining policy networks in EU governance. These contacts between the Commission and national ministries allow the member state to signal and frontload its positions and viewpoints into the policy proposals of the Commission through its SNEs. This, however, should not be interpreted as a direct national influence. Firstly, the Commission welcomes the experience, networks and input of the SNEs because the success of policy proposals depends on the member states themselves. SNEs also stress how loyal they are to the Commission during their secondment. Secondly, the influence is exercised fairly indirectly through the SNE's own thought processes which they characterise as having been shaped by their national background and upbringing. Thirdly, there is an entire chain of command before the SNE's draft proposal reaches the upper levels of the Commission where sections of the proposal may be modified. Finally, other than the distinction between national or EU interests, the role of expertise itself may be a third significant variable. Experts working within transnational networks develop distinct professional norms and values. Although this study does not take this factor into account, future contributions to this field could benefit from the inclusion of the role of expertise as a source of substantive preferences. On the whole, however, secondment seems still to be a legitimate and valued exchange system of officials for both the Commission and the member states.

However, our study has also demonstrated that not all of the hopes people have for the secondment system are fulfilled and the long-term benefits of these networks are often fairly limited, which can be perceived as an opportunity loss for the seconding member states. Many former SNEs do not land in jobs that allow them to draw upon their Commission networks; many do not return to their original home organisations.

Since networks are more dependent upon individuals than positions within an organisation, the enhanced trust and frank exchange may persist after someone changes position. The conditions under which this persistence is more or less likely to occur remains uncultivated research territory. These networks can facilitate decision-making by dispatching more and more national experts onto the supranational level and subsequently reabsorbing these same experts back into one's national administration (see Beyers and Kerremans 2004).

In this chapter, we have identified a number of mechanisms through which SNEs can potentially play a linking role between the Commission and the member state. The secondment system does indeed facilitate information flows and, in specific cases, influences an intricate web of relations across the formal institutional structures of the EU and its member states.

The results of the Dutch case, however, show that the SNEs are not optimally utilised. Even though the recent efforts of the Dutch government have led to increased levels of contact between the SNEs and their 'home base', there is still much room for improvement. When considering how the benefits of the secondment system can be made to endure after the secondment period, the career paths of the officials after their secondment are a crucial factor. At present, expertise and networks fade quickly as experts, quite literally, 'move on.' Better career planning for the SNEs would prevent this from happening and maximise the benefits for the member state.

CHAPTER 6

UNDERSTANDING EUROCRATIC WORK: CONCLUSIONS AND REFLECTIONS

6.1 Dutch Eurocracy revisited

The research reported in this study was prompted by the widely perceived shift from 'classic' to 'new' diplomacy in the very design and day-to-day practices of international regimes such as the European Union. We set out to examine what implications the rise of policy-oriented, domain-specific bilateral, as well as multilateral, diplomacy (noted in chapter 1) has had on how nation-states organise their relations with their regional neighbours and the web of international organisations they belong to or are engaged in. By focusing on the case of the Netherlands and its modus operandi in the European Union, we wanted to document how its executive branch practices the art of 'doing the government's business' at the international level. Over half a century of deepening and widening European integration has clearly led to an increased involvement of hitherto 'domestic' ministries and officials, but how large has this shift been, and what forms has it actually taken? In particular, we sought answers to the following three research questions:

1. To what extent are Dutch civil servants involved in EU-related activities?
2. How do individual Dutch civil servants experience and practise the craft of policy-making for and in European arenas?
3. How and to what extent are these civil servants facilitated and constrained by existing ways of organising European affairs in their respective organisations?

Each of these questions was specified in a number of more specific issues (see chapter 1 and below). In this final chapter, we review the findings regarding each of these issues, which we gathered through a range of complementary research methods. We summarise the main findings of the preceding empirical chapters with regard to each of the main research questions. We will also try to integrate the findings from the two surveys and the two qualitative case studies to draw a number of overarching conclusions. And we will confront our empirical findings with the outcomes of the expert meetings that were held in the final stages of the fieldwork phase of the project. These expert meetings were meant to provide a sounding board for our observations, allowing us to better assess the extent to which they were shared by people working on EU-related matters within a wide range of organisations in central government.

6.2 Eurocrats: How many, where?

Our comprehensive survey tracing the European involvement of Dutch civil servants (see chapter 2) yields a clear yet somewhat paradoxical conclusion: although nobody doubts the large and increased significance of the European Union for how the Netherlands is governed, the number of Dutch central government bureaucrats actively engaged in EU matters is still modest. Although overall a firm 30% of respondents indicated that their work is affected by the EU, by far most of them actually spend little time on EU-related activities. *Plus ça change, plus c'est la même chose.* EU-related work to date, although no longer the near-exclusive domain of Foreign Affairs and Agriculture officials, has remained somewhat of a specialised activity in Dutch central government. Doing the Dutch government's business in Brussels, with Brussels, or as a result of decisions made in Brussels, is a matter of pockets of specialists scattered around departments and agencies, not one of which involves a broad front of public servants.

The survey also revealed important differences in the levels of 'Europeanisation' among various central government organisations. Generally speaking, organisations in which more civil servants were involved in EU-related activities, also had respondents who spent more time on those activities and the activities tended to be dispersed more widely across the entire organisation, while the opposite held true for organisations with fewer Europeanised civil servants.

Hence, although the 'new diplomacy' covers a vast and increasing range of issues and policies that used to be purely domestic or even subnational government concerns, the number of fully engaged 'new diplomats' is modest by comparison. This finding may be somewhat surprising. Unfortunately, at present it is impossible to put it into a broader historical or cross-national comparative perspective. To our knowledge, no similar study has been conducted before in the Netherlands or anywhere else for that matter.

6.3 Eurocratic work: Individual professionalism

Our second major research question, regarding the Eurocratic practices of individual public servants, was broken down into six specific issues: their role orientations, their activity and contact patterns, the arenas and channels they use to do their business, how they see and use the rules of the European policy game, their standards of effectiveness (what constitutes a 'good day's work?' for a Eurocrat), and the knowledge and expertise they think Eurocrats need to possess in order to achieve their goals. Below we discuss our main findings concerning each of these issues.

Role orientations
The original question here was: what do national civil servants see as their chief tasks and goals when they participate in European policy processes? This study clearly shows that there are various ways of perceiving Eurocratic work, which conform to the three categories of Eurocrats discerned in chapter 4, and which can be grouped along a continuum ranging from 'business as usual' to the 'radical re-invention of policy work'. Those closest to the 'business as usual' end are those officials who resemble the back office co-ordinator ideal type. Their work is essentially in The Hague, and consists of working the levers of intradepartmental and interdepartmental consultation in order to facilitate coherent Dutch positions to fit into EU timetables (cf. Ekengren 2004). A more hybridised role conception can be found among a large majority of the *bureaucrat-diplomats*, who see themselves as having a dual role:

- In EU arenas, their role is to articulate and represent 'the Dutch interest' vis-à-vis other member-states and the European institutions;
- In the Netherlands, they see their role as 'selling' the EU to their colleagues and creating a better understanding of the possibilities and constraints inherent in European co-operation.

These people are intermediaries operating on the cutting edge of two worlds: the world of European co-operation and the world of national policy-making and its bureaucratic politics. These dual roles may conflict when there are clear tensions between Dutch preferences and the EU's policy directions. At the same time, various interviewees confided that they often use that tension creatively, telling constituents in one arena that they are under severe pressure from the other, and vice versa. The job is perhaps more difficult for bureaucrat diplomats operating in organisations where the overall degree of Europeanisation is low, and where 'doing business in Europe' is much less interesting or prestigious than 'doing business in The Hague.' They face constant scepticism from colleagues as well as their direct superiors when they try to raise their awareness of the significance of the EU to the work of their section – let alone when they're trying to argue the case for investing more time, expertise and money in the development of a serious EU presence.

On the other end of the continuum, most *street-level entrepreneurs* within departments and executive agencies see their roles at the European/international level as an opportunity for policy innovation. The generic drive to 'get things done' with regard to concrete needs, problems and opportunities arising at the 'shop floor' level of policy implementation and service delivery leads these actors to play down their roles as representatives of the 'Dutch' position in favour of their 'practical professionalism' when engaging their peers in the Commission or those from other countries. They operate in settings where the rules of the game are less dense and fixed, and cherish the opportunities of unorthodox, innovative, joint problem-solving that this entails.

These observations tie in with the literature, which shows that participants in EU decision-making situations tend to oscillate between representing national positions on the one hand, and embracing the core beliefs and

	Back office co-ordinators	Bureaucrat-diplomats	Street-level entrepreneurs
Key strengths	Facilitate emergence of timely and coherent departmental and national positions	Skilful negotiators for national positions while minimising Dutch opportunity costs of European integration	Practical professional problem solvers exploiting opportunities for transnational co-operation
Key weaknesses	Immersed in domestic bureaucratic politics, out of touch with EU-level and on the ground realities	Status-quo players immersed in the procedural politics of European policy processes	Out-of-control hobbyists with no grasp of the 'main game' of European integration and the need for an integrated national approach to playing it

Table 6.1 Strengths and weaknesses of Eurocratic ideal types

ambitions of their professional policy domain, on the other (for example, Thedvall 2006). Moreover, our study confirms the conclusion from earlier research that purely supranational (i.e., EU-related) loyalties tend to be scarce among national civil servants because their allegiance is primarily with their own government and/or policy area (cf. Suvarierol 2007). Our study adds to this current literature by identifying the predominant role conceptions that certain types of civil servants have, who, we argue, tend to each operate within specific types of international policy networks.

The contrast drawn in chapter 4 between the three types of civil servants, but particularly between bureaucrat-diplomats and street-level entrepreneurs, is an ideal-typical one. We do not argue, for example, that no Eurocrats with street-level entrepreneurial role orientations are found in 'First Pillar' settings, and vice versa. In reality, the picture is more mixed. However, it is useful to keep the pure types in mind, and reflect on their potential strengths and weaknesses.

For example, as table 6.1 shows, bureaucrat-diplomats risk ending up as essentially conservative, national or even departmental status-quo players focused more on the formal and diplomatic exigencies of European policy-making than on the potential gains of deeper integration and the pragmatic possibilities of professional problem solving. Street-level entrepreneurs, by contrast, have to be careful not to be seen as professional 'hobbyists' who use their roles as Dutch representatives in expert committees to indulge in hobby-like activities with like-minded foreign experts, whilst eluding hierarchical controls that are designed to induce them to represent Dutch rather than collegial outlooks and interests with regard to the matters at hand.

The activity and contact patterns of Eurocrats

The three general clusters of Europeanised civil servants were reflected in the results of the comparative case study into the veterinary and police co-operation domains. In the area of veterinary policy, interviewees found it difficult to distinguish between time allotted to EU-related and non-EU-related activities, since their policy area has been thoroughly Europeanised. As a result, 'EU-related' and 'domestic' policies and activities have become intertwined and concrete activities relate to both levels simultaneously. This is not only true for the relation between the EU-level and the domestic level: veterinary policy is also embedded in global networks, blurring the distinction between the EU and the global level. In police co-operation, the distinction between 'domestic' and 'EU-level' work is much clearer. Large parts of police work and criminal policy are firmly domestic in scope. As a result, officials in the field of police co-operation tend to differentiate more sharply between activities that relate to each of these levels. Within the field of police co-operation, the extent of involvement in EU-related activities depends on one's position within the organisation. EU-related activities appear to be allocated to a small number of specialised officials who have made it their main job. For them, EU-related activities take up a considerable part of their work, whereas for others it is only a minor or negligible part of their daily work.

In terms of contact patterns – what working on EU-related matters actually entails in terms of the ways public servants spend their time – another distinction emerges. Some officials operate on the 'front line' of contacts with officials from other governments and EU institutions. This group encompasses both the bureaucrat-diplomats and the street-level entrepreneurs of chapter 4. Departmental co-ordination bureaucrats, in contrast, occupy a 'back office' position. They co-ordinate EU-related work inside their own departments and in relation to other departments, but rarely engage in direct contacts with foreign counterparts themselves. They mainly interact with their departmental colleagues (including the departmental liaison at the Permanent Representation in Brussels) as well as with their counterparts from other ministries.

The two types of jobs are very different in terms of activities and required skills, but both are relevant in terms of understanding the patterns of activities in the EU and in Dutch central government. Every member-state needs 'Eurocratically astute' street-level entrepreneurs and bureaucrat-diplomats; but also well-resourced and effectively 'joined-up' EU co-ordination bureaucrats in every department.

Arenas and channels for Eurocratic work

Where does 'European' policy-making 'happen' for Dutch civil servants? Again, the answer is a qualified one. Where their European work takes them depends on what kind of job civil servants have. As the survey showed, most civil servants who deal with the EU do so in terms of policy implementation and transposition or are confronted with EU policies in making domestic policies. A smaller number of civil servants are involved in EU policy-making processes, be it directly in European forums or indirectly in the process of preparing and co-ordinating the Dutch input into EU decision-making.

The activities of civil servants involved in EU policy-making were the focus of our case studies. Based on these cases, we can discern three main 'loci' of EU-related policy-making activities. For *co-ordination bureaucrats*,

European policy-making happens in The Hague. They are the central figures in (inter)departmental networks that are involved in EU policy-making
and/or the implementation of EU law and policies. For *bureaucrat-diplomats*, European policy-making happens in Brussels. They go to committee,
working group and high-level meetings in Brussels and meet colleagues
there. In the case of police co-operation, which falls under the EU's Third
Pillar, contacts with foreign counterparts outside of these formal meetings
are comparatively rare. In veterinary policy, which falls under the EU's First
Pillar, contacts also take place outside of the formal meetings in order to
form decision-making coalitions in the committee.

Finally, for Dutch *street-level entrepreneurs*, European policy-making can
happen anywhere in Europe. These officials are actively engaged in forming networks with foreign counterparts in order to exchange information,
enhance mutual understanding, and undertake joint actions in response to
commonly experienced problems. These informal networks and their joint
activities may be formalised in EU decision-making forums, but often this
is not the case, or EU actors only come in as targets for lobby activities, spon-
sors or simply 'people to talk to.'

Formal and informal rules of the Eurocratic game

How does policy-making unfold in these arenas? The literature on EU committees has pointed out that different policy-making arenas within the EU
operate under different rules and that these differences matter for how their
participants can operate within them. As demonstrated in chapter 4, Council Working Parties emphasise the nationality of participants much more,
leading to stronger 'national' role perceptions by member-state representatives. Whereas in Commission expert groups, national backgrounds are
de-emphasised, leading to a stronger identification of the participants with
the EU or their professional roles. Furthermore, prior research has emphasised that institutional changes to the EU fabric such as enlargement and
the diffusion of co-decision procedures have seriously affected the incen-
tive structures of individual member-states and their representatives.

Our study echoes these findings insofar as it pertains to these formal EU
arenas. During the expert meetings, several participants noted that the ad-
vent of co-decision in their issue areas has meant that they are now chan-
nelling more efforts into lobbying MEPs than they used to. The same goes
for the outreach to national parliamentarians: as national parliaments are
brought more and more into the loop of European policy-making, national
Eurocrats (will have to) adjust their support-building strategies.

In sum, the officials interviewed and observed in this study emphasised how the context within which they operate shapes their behaviour in different ways:

- The main basis for engaging with foreign counterparts. Formal EU arenas have acquired their own institutional momentum and encourage and constrain particular practices by national Eurocrats. At the same time, officials operating in Third Pillar and/or implementation settings emphasise the pivotal role played by informal networks, driven not by formal decision rules but by strongly motivated, proactive individuals from various countries and the 'coalitions of the willing' they are constantly seeking to build and maintain.
- The implicit understanding of participants in terms of which roles Eurocrats should play when and where, and which roles they can expect their domestic and foreign counterparts to play. These expectations pertain, among others, to the (de)emphasis of national, departmental and professional identities and loyalties, or to the allocation of attention to particular arenas, networks and relationships at the European level.
- The domestic co-ordination process prior to and following European meetings: departments oscillate between centralised and decentralised models of co-ordinating their EU-related work, choices which obviously influence the discretion and support experienced by individual Eurocrats.

Different loci of European decision may vary in terms of these elements, as highlighted by the comparison of beliefs and practices of civil servants in the veterinary and policing fields, respectively. The former were clearly focused on the Commission-led process of proposal development and formal decision-making that characterises First Pillar contexts. In the latter, especially street-level entrepeneurs, operating in the less institutionalised, more pluralistic Third Pillar context naturally gravitated more towards informal networking as a predominant mode of doing business in Europe.

The expert meetings confirmed this picture. The closer officials are to formal EU decision-making and the more closely they are integrated into the departmental organisation in The Hague, the more formalised the rules of the game will be and the more strongly these officials will see themselves as representing the interests of the Netherlands as a member-state and/or of their 'native' department. Likewise, the more peripheral officials and their operative domains are to formal EU decision-making and to the core international agenda of their departments, the less formalised the rules of mutual co-operation, the greater the discretion accorded to the individual issue experts, the greater the reliance on interpersonal ties between (often long-standing) members of ongoing expert committees, and the more strongly officials will see themselves as representatives of an international profession dealing with common, borderless problems.

Doing EU business well: Quality and effectiveness measures

What do Dutch civil servants consider to be 'a proper job' in operating on the European stage? In chapter 3, we started from the presumption that individual civil servants simply strive to achieve European policies that are in accord with the national preferences they are supposed to represent. Achieving these national preferences is the overriding measure of effectiveness. In chapter 4, we further disaggregated this general measure of effectiveness by empirically discerning two main views of success among the three types of civil servants working on EU-related activities. One considers success in terms of getting things on the agenda and factoring Dutch interests into EU decisions. This view is held by most back office co-ordinators and the bureaucrat-diplomats representing the Netherlands in formal EU decision-making arenas. The second view considers success in terms of solving (operational) problems of co-operation with foreign counterparts. This view is held by the bulk of the more operational bureaucrats who participate in expert and comitology committees and/or operate in more freewheeling emergent areas of EU activity.

These views reflect different ideas about the role, purpose and practical possibilities of European co-operation. They also reflect different work contexts within which these civil servants operate. Officials who hold a 'bureaucratic-diplomatic' view operate within a set of incentives and constraints that closely resembles the preoccupations of civil servants working on domestic issues within central government departments, which is contributing to the shaping of policy decisions and helping the minister to shine, or at least to avoid problems. It is particularly in policy areas that are fairly politicised at the European level that these classical imperatives of departmental bureaucratic life become more important.

Those who hold a 'street-level entrepreneurial view' tend to be faced with a different set of incentives and constraints that focuses much more on daily service delivery, which translates into a different set of criteria for quality and effectiveness. When the two worlds meet, there is often a certain degree of friction, as these different logics of EU policy-making are not necessarily easily aligned. Hence, entrepreneurial executive agency officials frequently expressed bemusement at the 'meddling' and 'limited added value' of the departmental middle managers they were forced to deal with. Likewise, departmental officials note that they were sometimes exasperated with the go-at-it-alone instincts of operational experts, as well as with their 'inability to grasp the big picture' of European policy in a particular domain.

It should be noted that the expert group meetings provided somewhat of a corrective to this line of analysis. They harboured three lessons. First, the national position is not always clearly and unambiguously formulated, and the dynamics of EU meetings may be such that individual representatives have to make on-the-spot decisions about how to interpret the national position in as yet unanticipated contexts. Without a clear picture of what to maximise, maximisation becomes difficult and improvisation begins. To the extent that this is considered undesirable, efforts should be made to provide Eurocrats with more, such as more detailed but above all 'smarter' (clear yet versatile) instructions and guidelines on what to aim for under various contingencies during the negotiation processes in and around EU meetings.

Second, the motivation structures of Eurocrats are more complex than simply achieving their goals. Grand statements about 'representing the national interest' do not hold sway in the complex realities of EU policy-making. The expert meeting participants have agreed that civil servants' perceptions of their own aims – and thus the criteria for judging whether they perform effectively in their roles – may be a matter of 'where one stands' with respect to the issues and policy domain at hand. Where one stands is, as always, partly determined by where one 'sits' in the larger fabric of the organisation: strategic departmental actors go for 'big pictures' and are willing to make complex trade-offs; operational experts feel they succeed only when European policies produce workable and helpful 'street-level' practices.

Furthermore, the aims of Eurocrats are influenced by issue characteristics, e.g., concrete ones that are dealt with in discrete and reasonably speedy processes versus complex ones that evolve gradually in fuzzy and drawn-out processes. In the former instance, the predominant criterion for success can and should be the extent to which Dutch preferences can be found in the eventual EU outcomes (policies, standards, rules, time tables, budget allocations), as implied in chapter 3. However, actual success is much more difficult to assess, particularly in the short run. Several next-best criteria were proposed during the expert meetings, ranging from simply getting one's voice heard during meetings; being taken seriously by the Commission and/or other member-states in the relevant EU arenas; and, more ambitiously, controlling the (evolving) framing of the issues on the agenda of the relevant EU arenas.

Finally, what can be aimed for is also determined by the strategic political stakes involved. One distinction kept popping up. There are 'defensive' issues, where the strategic aim is to prevent EU policies from coming into being that require changes to existing and valued Dutch ones. And there are also 'offensive' issues where the aim is to further the adoption of certain EU measures seen as advantageous to Dutch interests. In both cases Dutch Eurocrats have to engage in advocacy work, but clearly trying to block, delay or modify something presupposes a different set of trade-offs and tactics than trying to make something happen.

Eurocratic 'need to haves': Knowledge and expertise
What do civil servants who work intensively in the EU domain regard as crucial professional competencies for operating on the European stage? When asked about crucial competencies, interviewees came up with a list of obvious but clearly pivotal items:

- One should be able to operate in networks. 'People skills' are important in this regard;
- One should have a solid understanding of how the European arena works: the formal as well as the informal rules of the European governance game;
- One should speak at least one foreign language well but preferably more.
- One should be able to empathise with and 'read' one's foreign counterparts, e.g., by being well informed about their various national systems, practices and policy priorities.

Surprisingly, in both the interviews and the expert meetings even the most experienced Eurocrats play down the specific nature of the knowledge and expertise required at the European level when compared to the national level. Of course, they say, there is some specific knowledge about European governance structures and policy processes that people who work in or with 'Brussels' need to have, but acquiring this knowledge is considered to be no big deal. Any capable civil servant should be able to learn most of this quickly. Likewise, language skills are sometimes mentioned as a great asset but, significantly, a lack of multilingualism is not generally seen as debilitating effective operating in the EU (particularly in the more formal decision arenas). This observation is also borne out by the results of the survey, in which respondents evaluated the facilities for training most positively among the six statements on the organisational context of EU-related work.

Virtually all of the officials we observed and interviewed emphasised that the real key lies in generic networking skills (sociability, empathy, reciprocity, reliability), and add that in this regard there are no fundamental differences between what is required 'in Europe' and what is required in The Hague and environs. They did note that not everyone possesses these skills. All recounted instances of having worked in EU settings with Dutch colleagues who clearly lacked some of these essential qualities – and duly created problems for themselves and for the Dutch position. These experiences were not very frequent, however, and in many cases a 'quiet word' was sent back via the appropriate channels to their superiors, encouraging them to find replacements or get the individuals involved to lift their game.

These findings may of course be read in two different ways, depending upon one's own vantage point and preconceptions. They can be taken as a much-needed 'demystification' of Eurocratic civil service work, breaking through the conspiracy of insiders and calling into question the key role that the Foreign Office tends to see for itself in the European domain. Yet they can also be interpreted as evidence of the casual, off-handed, almost cavalier approach that Dutch civil servants apparently take towards the role of training and skill development in enhancing their capability to operate effectively in European policy processes.

6.4 Eurocratic work: organisational preconditions

Our second major question in chapter 1 related to the organisational context within which civil servants operate. We broke that question down into three segments – personnel policies, organisational structures and co-ordination processes – each of which entailed a number of more specific sub-themes discussed below.

How big a part of the job?
Do civil servants feel they have sufficient time and opportunity to devote themselves to the European dimension of their portfolio? As indicated above, the survey showed that EU-related activities are either an integral part of the activities in one's organisation and job or concentrated in a limited number of specialised officials within the department. In either case, the question is not so much whether individual jobs allow sufficient time to be

devoted to EU-related activities but whether EU-related activities are integrated into the departmental work in such a way that the *organisation* devotes sufficient attention to them. The correlation is evident: the various officials who noted during interviews that they felt they should devote more time to European issues and arenas tended to work in organisations (or parts of organisations) where such activities did not enjoy a high priority.

Likewise, the survey findings reported in chapter 2 revealed a consistent relationship between the degree of Europeanisation and the priority accorded to EU-related work in an organisation. Based on the three-fold distinction between 'Eurocratic bulwarks' (highly Europeanised organisations), 'Eurocratic runners-up' (moderately Europeanised) and 'national champions' (barely Europeanised), we found that the more highly Europeanised an organisation was, the higher the priority accorded to EU-related work. Moving from the empirical to the evaluational, an important question is whether 'national champions' devote *too* little attention to the EU. If so, it would be tempting to label these organisations 'Eurocratic laggards' (in neat semantic contrast with the two other clusters of Eurocratic bulwarks and Eurocratic runners-up), but this would be unfair. We ended up calling them 'national champions' to reflect the reality that these departments/ agencies tend to bear responsibility for policy portfolios that at present are simply not Europeanised. Like any other organisation in Europe, public or private, they too are bound by EU law in many and important aspects of their operation. As such, they need to have a degree of awareness and skill in dealing with the consequences of that reality. But to the extent that these organisations do not really have a core role in making or implementing EU policy, their low degree of Europeanisation does not necessarily reflect a parochial or backward attitude. It is simply a logical by-product of the institutional division of responsibilities and powers in their portfolio domains.

A solid career path?

To what extent are placements in Europe and posts that have a strong European component considered to be 'good career moves' in Dutch departments and agencies? The survey revealed important differences in this regard between respondents in 'Eurocratic bulwarks' on the one hand, and respondents in less Europeanised organisations on the other. Civil servants in Eurocratic bulwarks indicated much more frequently that experience with EU-related activities offered an advantage for their career development than civil servants in other types of organisations.

Similar differences emerged between the departments we studied in the two case studies. In the Ministry of Agriculture, which we included in the case study on veterinary policy, having European experience is considered to be good for one's career. This ministry distinguishes itself by an active placement policy to place people with European experience in important positions within the ministry. European experiences are therefore an integral part of one's career development, and the ministry actively seeks to integrate these experiences in its human resource management policies. At the other end of the spectrum, in the Ministry of Health, which was included in the veterinary policy case study, and the Ministry of the Interior, which was included in the police co-operation case, European experience is much less valued in the career development of officials. In these departments it was even felt that a spell at the EU-level could be an impediment to one's further career and that officials themselves actively had to search for a new position after having worked in Brussels and wanting to return to The Hague. The same was true for officials working within the police organisation, although several key police interviewees said there were clear signs of a change there towards an 'upgrading' of European/international job experiences.

Overall, the role of European experiences in the career development of individual civil servants appears to be directly linked to the priority accorded to EU affairs by the political and administrative leadership of a department (see further below). But as the expert meetings revealed, even in highly Europeanised departments ('EU bulwarks' in chapter 2) factoring in European expertise and placements abroad into human resource management in general and management development policies in particular prove to be a tough nut to crack. Several key challenges were identified.

First there is the 'out of sight out of mind' risk. Departments may 'lose sight' of the civil servants seconded to posts in Brussels and elsewhere. Not so much in a policy sense – departments are increasingly organising 'comeback sessions' for all their staff placed abroad to compare notes, co-ordinate policy positions and to convey departmental priorities – but in a career planning sense. People lose track of how long someone's secondment was and how long they have already been away for. Directors looking to fill positions will be more aware of people they see on a regular basis, and there are few institutional mechanisms of reminding them that there are possible candidates for the job currently working abroad. The same goes vice versa, of course. Many Eurocrats sent to Brussels (as an SNE or at the Permanent Representation) get drawn into their new lives, acquire a taste for operating in the fast lanes of the EU and other foreign capitals, and may begin to bank on sticking around. As a result, they may not be as proactive in maintaining the informal networks in their home ministries needed to keep their careers afloat. As a result, the survey among SNEs that was reported on in chapter 5 shows that more than one-third of all former Dutch SNEs no longer work at the organisation that had originally sent them, while less than 30% still regularly use the networks they had developed during their stay in Brussels.

Secondly, there is a tendency to send out people who are 'too old', e.g., occupy relatively senior positions in the department. By definition, the number of jobs for them is smaller than for relatively junior staff, which makes them more difficult to place back into the department upon their return from abroad. The added complication is that at both lower and middle-management levels there is much less interdepartmental job mobility than at the highest levels. Many people's careers are focused within their own department. As a result of these factors, the average returnee from the EU circuit tends to fish in a relatively small pond. This being the case, each department has various cases of EU returnees who ended up stuck between a rock and a hard place career-wise. Stories about these cases circulate around the organisation, and provide a disincentive for others to go down the route of a European placement.

Acting with a clear mandate?

How are policy priorities to be achieved at the European level developed and communicated to the civil servants who operate in European arenas? What degree of discretion are they given? In the survey, respondents were asked whether they received a clear mandate when participating in EU-level meetings. Significantly, respondents in European bulwarks said they received clearer mandates than respondents in other types of organisations.

These survey results offer a broad-stroked picture of the perceived clarity of mandates among civil servants, but they hardly give an insight into the dynamics of mandate formation in day-to-day EU-related work. These dynamics emerged more clearly in the two case studies, however. In both of the case studies it was found that civil servants enjoyed a considerable degree of discretion in determining the Dutch position in European forums. Several officials indicated that they wrote their own mandates and that interference from higher political and administrative levels was limited. The backgrounds for this are somewhat different in the two cases. Veterinary policy is part of a close-knit expert community in which officials have considerable leeway in determining their own priorities and positions. As a result, officials experience only limited steering from the department's political and administrative leadership. In contrast, European police co-operation enjoys relatively low priority, particularly within the Ministry of the Interior. As a result, officials dealing with transborder policing, particularly police officers in the field, have considerable discretion to formulate their own positions and take their own initiatives. They were not particularly happy with this 'freedom', however, since they felt they lacked the strategic ministerial support needed to be effective at the EU-level. In the Ministry of Justice the degree of centralisation of EU policy formulation was considerably higher, partly because of the minister's personal interest, and partly because that ministry occupies the head of delegation role in several crucial European arenas in this policy domain.

To make sure all the bases are covered in the drawing up of instructions, most departments have now begun working with broad-based 'dossier teams' on issues deemed important by their leaderships. These teams are generally considered to be effective vehicles for exchanging information, co-ordinating a single and balanced departmental position, and being effective in the interdepartmental arena, where ultimately 'the' Dutch position ought to be negotiated (various participants noted that the producing of the latter can be an arduous task in the 'organised anarchy' of Dutch horizontal policy co-ordination). However, as with any solution to anything, it is not without potential problems of its own. Two stand out: at any point in time, one can have only so many of them, which raises the question of who decides on which grounds if an issue qualifies to be given this kind of systematic and sustained attention; and not each and every bundle of relevant expertise may be represented on the dossier teams (the often understaffed and overworked legal divisions of departments being a case in point).

Are Eurocrats held accountable?

How do civil servants who operate in European arenas report about their activities to their 'back offices', and do these ascertain and evaluate their performance? We can be brief here, since the answer to this question is related to the response to the question about instruction and guidance. Instruction and feedback run in tandem: without clear instructions there is no clear feedback mechanism. The main reason for this is that both are the result of priorities and interest from the departmental leadership. We will turn to this point next.

Does top management care?

To what extent do the upper echelons of the organisation accord priority to European issues, and to what extent do they get personally involved in European arenas if and when needed? The survey study showed that most civil servants feel that European issues enjoy low to moderate priority in their organisations, although there were clearly distinctions between various clusters of organisations.

In the case studies, it became clearer that top management commitment to EU affairs does vary greatly between departments. In the Ministry of Agriculture, the EU is part of its daily work and is therefore an integral part of the department's commitment and priorities. In the Ministry of Justice, EU affairs have gained greater importance because of the current minister's commitment to them. Still, EU activities are less integrated into this Ministry's day-to-day operations than in the Ministry of Agriculture. As a consequence, commitment from top management is much more contingent upon the personal or political choices of the top management than of organisational routines. In the Ministries of Health and the Interior, EU affairs have a relatively low priority. As a result, interest in and commitment to EU issues by top management is limited.

Discussions in the expert groups confirmed the idea that differences in top management's commitment to EU issues and activities can have significant consequences for Eurocratic work. Lack of commitment makes their work more difficult. Interviewees indicate that (active) political support from one's minister is crucial to get something done. This is true both at the EU-level proper (e.g., when a minister is willing to make a phone call to a colleague from another member-state in order to speed up decision-making or generate support for the Dutch position) and in relations with other departments in the Netherlands. Lack of commitment leads to a peripheral position for officials working on EU affairs within the department. This again has two consequences. It means that EU activities are separated from other, 'domestic' activities in the department. The EU becomes an add-on to the department's activities, rather than an integral part of it. It means that European experiences hardly play a role in the department's policies toward career development of individual civil servants (see also above).

It was also noted that management commitment is not just about management rhetoric – these days, no sensible department leader will deny the importance of the EU in the affairs of his organisation – but about management also 'walking the talk' in terms of its role in setting strategic priorities, allocating its personal attention to EU dossiers when needed, demonstrating by example, personal ambition and competence in the European domain, and creating proper incentives for staff to do the same.

Are Eurocrats well-resourced?

Do civil servants involved in European policy work find there is enough funding and staff support from their organisations for them to be able to operate effectively? As noted earlier, the answer to this question depends to a large degree on the way EU activities are integrated into a department's organisational routines. Where the EU is an integral part of a department's day-to-day work, there is very little distinction between domestic and EU-related activities, and issues of funding and staff support become part of more general debates about funding for specific government activities. Where the EU is a more isolated element in a department's activities, funding and staff support become more of an issue in themselves. The number of staff dedicated to EU-related activities then becomes a direct result of the relative importance accorded to EU issues by the departmental leadership. As stated above, the main problem then is not the low amount of funding and personnel available for EU-related tasks as such, but the lack of support for the Eurocrats in these organisations from other parts and higher levels of the organisation.

6.5 Grasping the real world of Eurocracy: The road ahead

This book has attempted to demonstrate the usefulness of studying European integration from the perspective of individual national civil servants or 'national Eurocrats'. They are the ones who 'make the EU happen' and whose activities shape EU policy-making on a daily basis. A lot of EU research and debate is squarely focused on ' big picture issues' of integration theory, but we believe that many developments in EU governance practices can be observed most closely by zooming in on the activities of these civil servants. By studying the way national Eurocrats operate within EU arenas as well as their domestic organisational contexts, one can obtain a clearer focus on some of the major questions and dilemmas of European integration and European governance: the impact of the EU on domestic governments and policy-making; the day-to-day realities of 'two-level games' and the tensions between 'the national' and 'the European' in EU governance; issues of authority, control, co-ordination and accountability in an executive branch facing a rapidly internationalising administrative and policy environment.

We have sought to show the promise and added value of this perspective, even if we have only been able to sketch some preliminary results of this kind of research programme. We do believe this study makes three significant contributions to the literature on European integration and EU governance. First, our study unveils a range of basic empirical insights into the extent and nature of Dutch national Eurocracy. We unveil and chart a Eurocratic world that until now has largely remained hidden. It provides a snapshot of the who, where and how much of the penetration of European issues and arenas into the work of national policy bureaucrats that complements similar attempts to look at the extent to which the need to implement EU legislation and guidelines occupies national administrations (Knill 2001; Mastenbroek 2007). Second, the study of Eurocratic practices has revealed an important distinction between types of civil servants dealing with the EU. The nature of Eurocratic work can be usefully understood in terms of these three types of public servant profiles: 'bureaucrat-diplomats' primarily working in highly formalised EU decision-making forums (and, incidentally the Eurocrats who are most likely to be actively engaged in the three types of pre-proposal stage, Commission-focused tactics described in detail in chapter 3); 'street-level entrepreneurs', primarily found in informal, task-related European policy networks; and those working in the 'back office' of The Hague departments, co-ordinating EU-related work within and across organisations ('departmental co-ordination bureaucrats'). It may be useful to expand that typology even further to also encompass the Brussels-based national Eurocrats, e.g., SNEs as well as those seconded to the Permanent Representation, although it is not immediately evident that they share much beyond their physical location at the heart of the EU polity. Clearly SNEs have to engage in a subtle balancing act that officials at the Permanent Representation do not. But they do share the fact that they have to survive in the Brussels milieu on a full-time instead of a 'yo-yoing' (Thedvall 2006) basis.

The distinction between these types of civil servants runs through almost all aspects of individual EU-related activities. As we have seen, it is relevant for their role orientations, for their daily activities and contact patterns, for the arenas in and channels through which they are active, for the formal and informal rules of the game they have to cope with, and for the measures of quality and effectiveness they apply. Distinguishing between types of Eurocrats is therefore crucial for understanding what kind of activities take place and why these activities are done the way they are. Moreover, this typology of civil servants highlights some key challenges in organising EU-related work within Dutch government. 'The' Dutch input in EU policy-making is formed by the combined efforts of all types of officials. More often than not, their respective activities focus on related concerns and have an impact on each other. At the same time, these types of civil servants have distinct outlooks on the EU and on the way EU-related work should be handled, making it highly likely that there will be both clashes and a lack of co-ordination. Hence, effectively organising EU-related activities largely consists of co-ordinating and accommodating these various activities so as to minimise overlap and tensions, and increase possible synergies.

Our third major finding that lends itself to further exploration in cross-national comparative studies pertains to the organisational context of Eurocratic work. The overriding differences found in our study relate to the degree of Europeanisation that public organisations display. The more highly Europeanised an organisation is, the higher the priority accorded to EU-related work, the better EU-related work is for one's career, and the better this work is organisationally facilitated. We called this the 'virtuous circle' of organisational Europeanisation, whereby greater degrees of Europeanisation lead to better organisational facilitation which may in turn be expected to strengthen EU-related work in the organisation again. This conclusion pinpoints key determinants of what one might call organisational EU competence: the degree to which EU-related issues and arenas are seen by top management to affect the organisation's core portfolios, and the degree to which this contributes to ensuring that the special requirements of facilitating Eurocratic work in terms of personnel policies, organisational structures and co-ordination routines are met.

If this hypothesis is able to withstand more rigorous scrutiny in cross-sectoral and cross-national empirical research, it has practical implications for efforts to improve the way EU-related work is organised and facilitated within national bureaucracies. The challenge from the top down becomes how to get the organisation to pass the 'critical threshold' that separates the 'Eurocratic bulwarks' from their counterparts where Eurocratic work leads a more marginal existence. When should the few remaining 'national champions' prepare themselves to join the ranks of the 'Eurocratic runners-up' and thus start to invest more heavily in freeing up and enabling their members to become more active in European arenas? This is not an easy call. Ten years ago, when the speed of the integration process was high, it seemed there was an 'EU domino effect' of sorts on the rise. It seemed only a matter of time before each and every hitherto national policy domain would be Europeanised. Not preparing for that onslaught would have been bad management. Nowadays, the pace has decreased, and the imperative to 'shape up' is perhaps somewhat less compelling. However, looking back at the long-term dynamics of European integration suggests that the process has always gone in spurts interrupted by impasses. We are now clearly at such an impasse, but if history is anything to go by in preparing for the future, the lesson here is that sooner or later there will be a further 'deepening' of the European Union. National departments and agencies currently not yet in the European front line would do well to anticipate this and continue to invest in capacity-building.

APPENDIX

ITEMS ON EUROPEANSATION INCLUDED IN THE 'POMO' SURVEY

PART H IMPACT OF THE EUROPEAN UNION
In your work you may be affected by the European Union (EU). For instance, you may be involved in preparing the Dutch input into EU decision-making, you may be participating in meetings at the EU level or bilateral meetings with colleagues from other member states, or you may play a role in implementing European legislation and policies. Some of these activities are listed in what follows.

1. Is your work affected by the European Union?

   ☐ *Yes*
   ☐ *No, go to question XXX.*

2. Can you indicate the importance of the following activities in your work?

	Totally un-important	Not very important	Neutral	Fairly important	Very important
1. Preparation of the Dutch input into EU-level meetings	☐	☐	☐	☐	☐
2. Participation in working groups of the Council of Ministers	☐	☐	☐	☐	☐
3. Participation in meetings organised by the European Commission (e.g. expert meetings, comitology)	☐	☐	☐	☐	☐
4. Consultation with colleagues from one or more other member states outside the formal EU framework.	☐	☐	☐	☐	☐
5. Transposition of European policies into national legal measures	☐	☐	☐	☐	☐
6. Practical application or enforcement of rules and policies that originated in the EU	☐	☐	☐	☐	☐
7. Taking into account EU policies during national policy-making	☐	☐	☐	☐	☐
8. Involving local government in EU-level decision-making or policy-making	☐	☐	☐	☐	☐

3. *On average, how many hours per week do you spend on the EU-related activities listed above?*

☐ ☐ hours per week (go to question XXX if you spend 0 hours per week on EU-related activities).

4. The following statements concern how your employer facilitates EU-related activities organisationally. This may involve training opportunities, career development or managerial support. To what extent do you agree with the following statements?

	I do not agree at all	I do not agree	Neutral	I agree	I totally agree	Don't know/not applicable
1. My organisation offers sufficient training opportunities for EU-related activities	☐	☐	☐	☐	☐	☐
2. When selecting candidates for EU-related activities, my employer sufficiently takes my European experience into account	☐	☐	☐	☐	☐	☐
3. Gaining experience in EU-related activities offers an advantage for my career	☐	☐	☐	☐	☐	☐
4. When I participate in EU-level meetings, I receive a clear negotiation mandate	☐	☐	☐	☐	☐	☐
5. In my organisation, EU-related activities have a lower priority than purely national activities	☐	☐	☐	☐	☐	☐
6. In my policy area there is sufficient co-ordination between those who negotiate at the EU-level about European policies, and those responsible for transposing and implementing those policies	☐	☐	☐	☐	☐	☐

NOTES

NOTES CHAPTER 1

1   We chose the Netherlands for purely pragmatic reasons because the authors lived there, and there was interest among Dutch officials in a study of their own 'Eurocratic practices'. We have no reason to assume that the Dutch case is in any way a 'crucial case' of national Eurocratic practices. If anything, evidence from similar studies in other countries suggest that there are many common features (see, e.g., SBOV 2004; Thedvall 2006).

2   Over the past number of years, a plethora of studies and governmental reports have analysed formal co-ordination mechanisms and proce- dures in Dutch government (Soetendorp and Andeweg 2001; de Zwaan 2005; Gemengde Commissie 'Sturing EU-Aangelegenheden' 2005; Raad van State 2005; Raad voor het Openbaar Bestuur 2004; Hanf and Soetendorp 1998). These studies and reports all focus on the co-ordination process that leads to the formulation of an official 'Dutch position' in EU decision-making processes. We do not aim to con- tribute to this debate. By contrast, our study looks at co-ordination and management in daily work practices, quite apart from the formal stages of EU decision-making.

NOTES CHAPTER 2

3   Because Norway is not an EU member, Egeberg and Trondal (1999) asked questions regarding both the EU and the EEA (European Eco- nomic Area) Agreement, because the EEA Agreement forms the pri- mary legal link between Norway and the EU proper.

4   Four respondents indicated numbers of hours spent on EU-related ac- tivities that exceeded 40 hours, with one respondent responding with a total of 82 hours. Since we can assume these higher figures reflect a

(nearly) full working week, these respondents have been added to the '40 hour' category. This does not substantially affect the figures for this category.

5 For a few respondents, the EU-related time allotment exceeds 100%. This may be due to the fact that they regularly work overtime, or that they have more than one job (since the contractual working time is calculated on the basis of the respondent's primary job).

6 Principal Component Analysis is closely related to factor analysis but uses a different statistical method to extract the factors/components.

7 The analysis was carried out on the original five answer categories for each specific activity. The factors were extracted using Principal Component Analysis. Factor rotation was carried out using direct oblimin, because all activities are correlated to some extent. Factors were extracted if their own values were greater than 1.0. Tests for multicollinearity and sample size adequacy all scored well above minimally required values.

8 For the sake of clarity, Table 7 uses the dichotomous variables of Table 5 again.

9 The dispersion index is calculated as $1 / (n * \Sigma v_i^2)$, in which v_i is the share of the i-th respondent in the total amount of time spent on EU-related work in an organisation, and n is the total number of respondents in that organisation. This formula is based on the formula for calculating the 'effective number of parties' in a parliament or election (see Laakso and Taagepera 1979). The effective number of parties is used as a measure to account not only for the actual number of parties but also their relative size. For instance, if there are three parties, where one has 50% of the votes and the other two each have 25%, the effective number of parties will be 2.67. This number reflects the fact that the party system contains three parties but in practice also resembles a two-party system. We can use the same formula to calculate the 'effective number of civil servants' working on EU-related activities in an organisation, based on the amount of time spent by each civil servant as a portion of the time spent on EU-related activities by all civil servants together in that organisation. By dividing the effective number by the total number of civil servants in that organisation, we obtain a figure of between 0 and 1.

10 This is the reason why we have restricted the calculation of the dispersion index to those respondents whose work is affected by the EU. If the dispersion index is calculated for all respondents (thus including respondents whose work is not affected by the EU), the dispersion index

is no longer independent of the overall level of EU involvement in an organisation.

11 The category 'Hoog College van Staat' includes, among others, the Dutch Council of State and support staff in Parliament.

12 Since the dispersion for this category is based on a very small number of civil servants, it cannot be compared very easily with other organisations in this table. Therefore, we have put the dispersion index in brackets.

13 The Ministry of General Affairs is the Prime Minister's Office.

14 Since the dispersion index for the Ministry of General Affairs is based on just two civil servants involved in EU-related work (each spending one hour per week on the EU), this figure cannot be compared well to those of other organisations in the table. Therefore, we have put it in brackets.

15 It should be noted that the Ministry of Justice in our survey also included support staff in the courts system. This may have suppressed the level of EU involvement we found, since the relative number of civil servants involved in EU-related work may be higher at the policy department in The Hague than in the courts. Unfortunately, the survey data do not allow us to make this distinction.

16 Correlations have been calculated using the time share of each respondent, that is, the number of hours spent on EU-related activities as a percentage of contractual working time.

17 Since respondents from the Tax Service comprise a large portion of the respondents in the 'moderate' category, we re-ran the analysis without the tax department. This reduced the differences between the moderate group and the others somewhat, but it did not reverse the order of these groups.

NOTES CHAPTER 3

18 We do not discuss a potential third stream of uploading studies here. The burgeoning literature on 'networked governance', 'new modes of governance', or 'democratic experimentalism' (Jordan and Schout 2006; Citi and Rhodes 2007; Sabel and Zeitlin 2007) examines the problems of co-ordination associated with managing the networks within policy areas emerging under the Open Method of Coordination. The achievement of any of the four key elements of the OMC – fixing guidelines and timetables, establishment of indicators and benchmarks, translation of these into European guidelines and their imple-

mentation at national and regional levels, and the periodic monitoring, evaluation and peer review of policies (Lisbon Presidency Council Conclusions, European Council 2000) – may qualify as a form of uploading – uploading by consent – but its discussion is beyond the focus of this chapter.

19 However, the question of how powerful the Commission is vis-à-vis the Council and European Parliament *during* the co-decision game is rife with debate. Whereas some argue that the Commission has become virtually toothless since the introduction of co-decision II (Tsebelis and Garrett 2000, 2001; Crombez 2001) others argue that conditions can emerge under which the Commission can play a substantial role (Scharpf 1999; Peterson 2002; Burns 2004; Schmidt 2000).

20 Writing on the situation before the Maastricht Treaty, i.e., before the introduction of the co-decision I procedure, Hull (1993) even argued that 80% of the text of Commission proposals survived the final stage of Council decision-making.

21 The section dealing with animal diseases and welfare within this ministry amounted to only 3.5 full-time employees who were influential at the time we conducted our interviews.

22 The Office International des Epizooties (OIE) is an intergovernmental organisation created by the International Agreement of 25 January 1924. In 1924, only 28 nations were members, currently there are over 160 members.

23 Group interviews with Eurocrats in focus groups corroborated the existence of these strategies. We can be fairly certain that frontloading, signalling and coalition-building strategies are common practices across a range of Europeanised ministries in the Dutch central government.

24 The Dutch Louise Fresco was FAO's Agricultural Department's Assistant Director General until 1 June 2006.

25 The informal circuit is, in any case, underexploited by Dutch civil servants. Brussels is too close to The Hague to stay overnight. Evening programmes, such as drinks and dinners, and meetings with fellow par-ticipants over breakfast at hotels, are generally missed by Dutch civil servants.

NOTES CHAPTER 5

26 The authors would like to thank Jarle Trondal for sharing his work and his questionnaires with us.

27 CLENAD UK Section (2002) *An Unofficial Guide for UK National Experts*, 3rd edition, p. 44-45.

28 One of the respondents had been seconded before this period but was included in the dataset to maximise the number of observations.

29 The survey was sent by e-mail, but the respondents were given a choice of returning the completed document electronically or by post.

30 It only became clear when data were gathered that two of the respondents had been detached prior to 2000. They have also been also included in the analyses given the value of empirical data.

31 The cross-time comparisons should also be read with caution, however, since the responses to survey questions with regard to the secondment period of former SNEs rely on their memory. An inevitable problem connected with research that relies on respondents' memories is the potential inaccuracy of the respondents' input.

32 The statistical figures concerning the Commission staff in this article are based on the European Commission *Statistical Bulletin of Commission Staff 04/2006*, the period of which corresponds to our data collection period.

33 *Commission Decision C(2004) 577 of 27 February 2004 laying down rules on the secondment of National Experts to the Commission*, Article 2.

34 CLENAD Nederlandse Sectie (2003), *Op naar een win³ situatie: Een overzicht voor de versterking van de banden tussen gedetacheerde medewerkers bij de Europese instelling en de overheid in Den Haag*, Brussels, p. 3.

35 *Commission Decision C(2004) 577 of 27 February 2004 laying down rules on the secondment of National Experts to the Commission*, p. 2.

36 Interview with SNE31, Brussels, Feb. 2006.

37 Caroline de Gruyter, 17-18 Jan. 2004, *NRC Handelsblad*, 'Banenjagen voor het Vaderland', p. 39.

38 Interview with SNE23, Brussels, Feb. 2006.

39 Interview with SNE84, The Hague, March 2006

40 Interview with SNE25, Brussels, Jan. 2006.

41 We adopted the same division as used by Liesbet Hooghe (2001) in *The European Commission and the Integration of Europe* to classify Commission Directorate-Generals according to policy areas.

42 We borrow Van der Meer and Raadschelders's classification (1999, 205-228), 'The Senior Civil Service in the Netherlands: A Quest for Unity', in Page and Wright (1999), *Bureaucratic Elites in Western European States*.

43 Interestingly, this observation is in direct contrast to the findings in

chapter 2, where we stated that 'higher ranks ... seem to be associated with higher levels of EU involvement'. One potential explanation for the divergent observation in the POMO survey is the clustering of all income levels above 5000 euro gross monthly into a single category, preventing the recording of variations between the seven different ranks that may fall into this one category.

44 Including one former SNE who had been seconded for five years.

45 We omitted the category 'Colleagues within your DG' for the basic reason that this category would be superfluous since all Commission officials have daily contacts with their colleagues.

46 The subcategories for Commission officials were omitted for the current contacts of former SNEs to enable a general overview of contacts with the Commission.

47 It is difficult, however, to conclude whether these exceptions are due to a real change in contact intensity or whether this divergence is merely a result of lower accuracy in the responses for which there is a reliance on the officials' memories.

48 Programma Andere Overheid, Rijksbrede takenanalyse, 2005, Gemengde Commissie 'Sturing EU-aangelegenheden' *Eindrapport*, The Hague, p. 12-13.

49 Gerben Everts quoted in *Den Haag kijkt teveel naar Den Haag*, PM 19/1, 2005, p. 27.

50 Interview with SNE79, The Hague, March 2006.

51 Interview with SNE20, Brussels, Feb. 2006.

52 Interview with SNE70, The Hague, March 2006.

53 Interview with SNE3, Brussels, Feb. 2006.

54 Interview with SNE18, Brussels, March 2006.

55 Interview with SNE23, Brussels, Feb. 2006.

56 Interview with SNE20, Brussels, Feb. 2006.

57 Interview with SNE31, Brussels, Feb. 2006.

58 Interview with SNE25, Brussels, Jan. 2006.

59 Interview with SNE61, Brussels, March 2006.

60 Interview with SNE20, Brussels, Feb. 2006.

61 Interview with SNE23, Brussels, Feb. 2006.

62 Interview with SNE84, The Hague, March 2006.

63 Interview with SNE63, The Hague, March 2006.

64 Interview with SNE145, The Hague, March 2006.

65 Interview with SNE79, The Hague, March 2006.

66 Interview with SNE70, The Hague, March 2006.

67 Interview with SNE25, Brussels, Jan. 2006.

68 Interview with SNE19, Brussels, March 2006.

69 Interview with SNE63, The Hague, March 2006.

70 This is not to say that the returning SNEs, as individuals, do not benefit from their experiences and networks, but the crucial point here is that the gains for the seconding organisation are limited if the SNEs leave the organisation upon their return home from their assignments at the Commission.

71 Interview with SNE66, The Hague, March 2006.

72 Interview with SNE84, Rotterdam, March 2006.

73 Interview with SNE25, Brussels, Jan. 2006.

74 Interview with SNE20, Brussels, Feb. 2006.

75 Interview with SNE35, Brussels, Feb. 2006.

76 Interview with SNE79, The Hague, March 2006.

77 The categories for answering this question were 'to a large degree', 'to a reasonable degree', 'to a limited degree', 'no', and 'rather the opposite', which were dichotomised into 'Yes' (the first 3 categories) and 'No' (the latter 2 categories).

78 Interview with SNE23, Brussels, Feb. 2006.

79 CLENAD (2003), Report of the Working Group 'Life after SNE?'.

BIBLIOGRAPHY

Babbie, E. (1992) *The Practice of Social Research*. Belmont: Wadsworth Publishing Company.

Baetens, M. and Bursens, P. (2004a) 'De Europeanisering van Bestuurlijke Structuren: Coördinatie en Implementatie van Europees Landbouw- en Milieubeleid in Vlaanderen', in: G. Bouckaert (coordinatie), *Vlaanderen en/in Europa: Omgaan met de Unie en Vergelijkend Leren*, SBOV Jaarboek 2004. Leuven: Die Keune, pp. 183-219.

Baetens, M. and Bursens, P. (2004b) 'De Europeanisering van de Bestuurlijke Cultuur: Europese Opinies en Aandacht van Vlaamse Ambtenaren en Politici', in: G. Bouckaert (coordinatie), *Vlaanderen en/in Europa: Omgaan met de Unie en Vergelijkend Leren*, SBOV Jaarboek 2004. Leuven: Die Keune, pp. 221-245.

Berridge, G.R. (2002) *Diplomacy: Theory and Practice*. Basingstoke: Palgrave.

Beyers, J. (2005) 'Multiple Embeddedness and Socialisation in Europe: The Case of Council Officials'. *International Organisation*, vol. 59, no. 4, pp. 899-936.

Beyers, J. and Kerremans, B. (2004) 'Bureaucrats, Politicians, and Societal Interests: How is European Policy-making Politicised?'. *Comparative Political Studies*, vol. 37, no. 1, pp. 1-31.

Beyers, J. and Trondal, J. (2004) 'How Nation States "Hit" Europe: Ambiguity and Representation in the European Union'. *West European Politics*, vol. 27, no. 5, pp. 919-942.

Börzel, T. (2002) 'Pace-Setting, Foot-Dragging, and Fence-Sitting: Member State Responses to Europeanisation'. *Journal of Common Market Studies*, vol. 40, no. 2, pp. 193-214.

Börzel, T. and Risse, T. (2000) 'When Europe Hits Home: Europeanisation and Domestic Change', *European Integration online Papers*, vol. 4, no. 15, available at <http://eiop.or.at/eiop/texte/2000-015a.htm>.

Bovens, M.A.P. (1998) *The Quest for Responsibility: Accountability and Citizenship in Complex Organisations.* Cambridge: Cambridge University Press.

Bovens, M.A.P. and Yesilkagit, K. (2005) 'De Invloed van Europese Regels op de Nederlandse Wetgever'. *Nederlands Juristenblad*, vol. 80. no. 10, pp. 520-529.

Brandsma, G.J. (2006) 'Position Paper: Accounting for Expert Input in European Policy-making', Unpublished Manuscript. Utrecht School of Governance: Utrecht University.

Burns, C. (2004) 'Codecision and the European Commission: A Study of Declining Influence?'. *Journal of European Public Policy*, vol. 11, no. 1, pp. 1-18.

Castricum, C. (2006) Rijksbreed Europees HRM-beleid gewenst: 'Den Haag kijkt teveel naar Den Haag'. *PM*, vol. 2, no. 1, pp. 27-29.

Christiansen, T. and Kirchner, E. (eds.) (2000) *Europe in Change: Committee Governance in the European Union.* Manchester: Manchester University Press.

Citi, M. and Rhodes, M. (2007) 'New Modes of Governance in the EU: Common Objectives versus National Preferences'. *European Governance Papers (EUROGOV)*, no. N-07-01, <http://www.connex-network.org/eurogov/pdf/egp-newgov-N-07-01.pdf>.

CLENAD (2003) Report of the Working Group 'Life after SNE?'. Brussels.

CLENAD Nederlandse Sectie (2003) 'Op naar een win-win situatie: Een overzicht voor de versterking van de banden tussen gedetacheerde medewerkers bij de Europese instelling en de overheid in Den Haag'. Brussels.

CLENAD UK Section (2002) *An Unofficial Guide for UK National Experts*, 3rd ed. Brussels.

Coen, D. (1998) 'The European Business Interest and the Nation-State: Large Firm Lobbying in the European Union and Member States'. *Journal of European Public Policy*, vol. 18, no. 1, pp. 75-100.

Coolsaet, R. (1998) *The Transformation of Diplomacy at the Threshold of the New Millennium*, available at <http://pswserv1.ugent.be/rc/Nederlands/Artikels/IP/IPWatzwaarder.htm>.

Craig, C., George, A.L. and Lauren, P.G. (2006) *Force and Statecraft: Diplomatic Problems of Our Time.* Oxford: Oxford University Press.

Crombez, C. (2001) 'The Treaty of Amsterdam and the Co-Decision Procedure', in: G. Schneider and M. Aspinwall (eds.), *The Rules of Integration.* Manchester: Manchester University Press, pp. 101-22.

Eberlein, B. and Kerwer, D. (2004) 'New Governance in the European

Union: A Theoretical Perspective'. *Journal of Common Market Studies*, vol. 42, no.1, pp. 121-142.

Egeberg, M. (1999) 'Transcending Intergovernmentalism? Identity and Role Perceptions of National Officials in EU Decision-Making'. *Journal of European Public Policy*, vol. 6, no. 3, pp. 456-474.

Egeberg, M. and Trondal, J. (1999) 'Differentiated Integration in Europe: The Case of EEA Country, Norway'. *Journal of Common Market Studies*, vol. 37, no. 1, pp. 133-142.

Egeberg, M., Schaeffer, G.F. and Trondal, J. (2003) 'The Many Faces of EU Committee Governance'. *West European Politics*, vol. 26, no. 2, pp. 19-40.

Eising, R. and Kohler-Koch, B. (1999) 'Governance in the European Union: A Comparative Assessment', in: B. Kohler-Koch and R. Eising (eds.), *The Transformation of Governance in the European Union*. London: Routledge.

Ekengren, M. (2004) 'National Foreign Policy Co-ordination: The Swedish EU Presidency', in: W. Carlsnaes, H. Sjursen, B. White (eds.), *Contemporary European Foreign Policy*. London: Sage.

European Commission (2004) *Commission Decision C(2004) 577 of 27 February 2004 Laying Down Rules on the Secondment of National Experts to the Commission*. Brussels.

European Commission (2006) *Statistical Bulletin of Commission Staff 04/2006*. Brussels.

Featherstone, K. and Radaelli, C.M. (eds.) (2003) *The Politics of Europeanisation*. Oxford: Oxford University Press.

Gemengde Commissie Sturing EU-Aangelegenheden (2005) *Eindrapport*, The Hague, 7 June 2005.

George, A.L. and Bennett, A. (2005) *Case Studies and Theory Development in the Social Sciences*. Cambridge, MA: MIT Press.

Goetz, K. and Hix, S. (eds.) (2001) *Europeanized Politics? European Integration and National Political Systems*. London: Frank Cass.

Green-Cowles, M., Caporaso, J.A. and Risse, T. (eds.) (2001) *Transforming Europe: Europeanisation and Domestic Change*. Ithaca: Cornell University Press.

Gruyter, C. de (2004) 'Banenjagen voor het Vaderland'. *NRC Handelsblad*, 17-18 January 2004, p. 39.

Haas, P.M. (1989) 'Do Regimes Matter? Epistemic Communities and Mediterranean Pollution Control'. *International Organisation*, vol. 43, no. 3, pp. 377-403.

Haas, P.M. (1992) 'Introduction: Epistemic Communities and International Policy Coordination'. *International Organisation*, vol. 46, no.1, pp. 1-35.

Hamilton, K. and Langhorne, R. (1995) *The Practice of Diplomacy: Its Evolution, Theory and Administration*. London: Routledge.

Hanf, K. and Soetendorp, B. (eds.) (1998) *Adapting to European Integration: Small States and the European Union*. London: Longman.

Harmsen, R. (1999) 'The Europeanisation of National Administrations: A Comparative Study of France and the Netherlands'. *Governance*, vol. 12, no. 1, pp. 81-113.

Hart, P. 't, Wille, A.C., Boin, R.A., van der Meer, F., Dijkstra, G. and Zannoni, M. (2002) *Politiek-Ambtelijke Verhoudingen in Beweging*. Amsterdam: Boom.

Haverland, M. (2000): 'National Adaptation to European Integration. The Importance of Institutional Veto Points'. *Journal of Public Policy*, vol. 20, no. 1, pp. 83-103.

Héritier, A., Knill, C., and Mingers, S. (1996) *Ringing the Changes in Europe: Regulatory Competition and the Transformation of the State*. Berlin: de Gruyter.

Hix, S. (2002) *The Political System of the European Union*. Basingstoke: Palgrave.

Hocking, B. and Spence, D. (eds.) (2002) *Foreign Ministries in the European Union: Integrating Diplomats*. London: Palgrave.

Hooghe, L. (1996) *Cohesion Policy and European Integration: Building Multilevel Governance*. Oxford: Oxford University Press.

Hooghe, L. (2001) *The European Commission and the Integration of Europe*. Cambridge: Cambridge University Press.

Hull, R. (1993) 'Lobbying Brussels: A View from Within', in: S. Mazey and J. Richardson (eds.), *Lobbying in the European Community*. New York: Oxford University Press, pp. 82–92.

Jacobsson, B., Lægreid, P. and Pedersen, O.K. (2004) *Europeanisation and Transnational States: Comparing Nordic Central Governments*. London: Routledge.

Jacobsson, B., Lægreid, P. and Pedersen, O.K. (eds.) (2001) *Europaveje: EU i de nordiske centralførvaltninger*. København: Jurist- og Oekonomforbundet.

Jönsson, C. and Strömvik, M. (2005) 'Negotiations in Networks' in: O. Elgström and C. Jönsson (eds.), *European Union Negotiations: Processes, Networks and Institutions*. London: Routledge, pp. 13-28.

Jönsson, C., Bjurulf, B., Elgström, O., Sannestedt, A. and Strömvik, M. (1998) 'Negotiations in Networks in the European Union'. *International Negotiation*, vol. 2, no.3, pp. 319-44.

Jordan, A. (2001) 'The European Union: An Evolving System of Multi-level Governance or Government?'. *Policy and Politics*, vol. 29, no. 2, pp. 193-208.

Jordan, A., and Schout, J.A. (2006) *The Coordination of the European Union: Exploring the Capacities of Networked Governance*. Oxford: Oxford University Press.

Kassim, H. (2001) 'Introduction: Co-ordinating National Action in Brussels', in: H. Kassim, A. Menon, B.G. Peters and V. Wright (eds.), *The National Coordination of EU Policy. The European Level*. Oxford: Oxford University Press, pp. 1-47.

Kassim, H. (2003) 'Meeting the Demands of EU Membership: The Europeanisation of National Administrative Systems', in: K. Featherstone and C.M. Radaelli (eds.), *The Politics of Europeanisation*. Oxford: Oxford University Press, pp. 83-111.

Kassim, H., Menon, A., Peters, B.G. and Wright, V. (eds.) (2000) *The National Co-ordination of EU Policy: The Domestic Level*. Oxford: Oxford University Press.

Kassim, H., Menon, A., Peters, B.G. and Wright, V. (eds.) (2001) *The National Coordination of EU Policy. The European Level*. Oxford: Oxford University Press.

Kennan, G.F. (1997) 'Diplomacy without Diplomats?'. *Foreign Affairs*, vol. 76, no. 5, pp. 198-207.

Knill, C. (2001) *The Europeanisation of National Administrations: Patterns of Institutional Change and Persistence*. Cambridge: Cambridge University Press.

Kohler-Koch, B. and Eising, R. (eds.) (1999) *The Transformation of Governance in the European Union*. London: Routledge.

Laakso, M. and Taagepera, R. (1979) 'Effective Number of Parties. A Measure with Application to West Europe'. *Comparative Political Studies*, vol. 12, no. 1, pp. 3-27.

Lægreid, P., Smari Steinthorsson, R. and Thorhallsson, B. (2004) 'Europeanisation of Central Government Administration in the Nordic States'. *Journal of Common Market Studies*, vol. 42, no. 2, pp. 347-369.

Laffan, B. and O'Mahoney, J. (2007) 'Managing Europe from an Irish Perspective: Critical Junctures and the Increasing Formalisation of the Core Executive in Ireland'. *Public Administration*, vol. 85, no. 1, pp. 167-188.

Larsson, T. (2003) *Pre-Cooking in the European Union: The World of Expert Groups*. Stockholm: ESO-report.

Larue, T. (2006) *Agents in Brussels: Delegation and Democracy in the European Union*. Ph.D. Dissertation, Department of Political Science, Umeå University.

Marks, G., Hooghe. L., and Blank, K. (1996) 'European Integration from the 1980s: State-centric versus Multi-level Governance'. *Journal of Common Market Studies*, vol. 34, no. 3, pp. 341-378.

Mastenbroek, E. (2007). *The Politics of Transposition: Explaining the Transposition of EC Directives in the Netherlands*. Wageningen: Ponsen & Looijen.

Mayer, F.W. (1992) 'Managing Domestic Differences in International Negotiations: The Strategic Use of Internal Side-Payments'. *International Organisation*, vol. 46, no. 4, pp. 793-818.

Mazey, S. and Richardson, J. (1993) *Lobbying the European Community*. Oxford: Oxford University Press.

McCubbins, M.D. and Schwartz, T. (1984) 'Congressional Oversight Overlooked: Police Patrols versus Fire Alarms', *American Journal of Political Science*, vol. 28, no. 1, pp. 165-179.

Meer, F.M. van der and Raadschelders, J.C.N. (1999) 'The Senior Civil Service in the Netherlands: A Quest for Unity', in: E.C. Page and V. Wright (eds.), *Bureaucratic Elites in Western European States*. Oxford: Oxford University Press, pp. 204-228.

Melissen, J. (ed.) (2006) *The New Public Diplomacy: Soft Power in International Relations*. Houndmills Basingstoke Palgrave MacMillan.

Noordegraaf, M. (2000) *Attention!*. Rotterdam: Eburon.

Page, E. and Jenkins, W.I. (2005) *Policy Bureaucracy*. Oxford: Oxford University Press.

Page, E.C. and Wright, V. (eds.) (1999) *Bureaucratic Elites in Western European States: A Comparative Analysis of Top Officials*. Oxford: Oxford University Press.

Pahre, R. (1997) 'Endogenous Institutions in Two-Level Games and Parliamentary Oversight of the European Union'. *Journal of Conflict Resolution*, vol. 41, no. 1, pp. 147-174.

Payne, D.C. (2000) 'Policy-Making in Nested Institutions: Explaining the Conservation Failure of the EU's Common Fisheries Policy'. *Journal of Common Market Studies*, vol. 38, no. 2, pp. 303-324.

Peters, B. G. and Pierre, J. (2001) 'Developments in Intergovernmental Relations: Towards Multi-level Governance'. *Policy and Politics*, vol. 29, no. 2, pp. 131-135.

Peters, B.G. and Wright, V. (2000) 'The National Co-ordination of European policy-making: Negotiating the Quagmire', in: J. Richardson (ed.),

European Union. *Power and Policy-Making*, 2nd ed. London: Routledge, pp. 155-178.

Peterson, J. (2002), 'The College of Commissioners', in: J. Peterson and M. Shackleton (eds.), *The Institutions of the European Union*. Oxford: Oxford University Press.

Programma Andere Overheid Rijskbrede takenanalyse (2005) Gemengde Commissie 'Sturing EU-aangelegenheden' *Eindrapport*, The Hague, 7 June 2005.

Putnam, R. (1988) 'Diplomacy and Domestic Politics: The Logic of Two-Level Games'. *International Organisation*, vol. 42, no. 3, pp. 427-460.

Raad van State (2005) *Advies no. W04.05.0338/I.* 15 September 2005.

Raad voor het Openbaar Bestuur (2004) *Nationale Coördinatie van EU-Beleid: Een Politiek en Proactief Proces*, Den Haag: ROB.

Rhinard, M. (2002) 'The Democratic Legitimacy of the European Union Committee System'. *Governance*, vol. 15, no. 2, pp. 185-210.

Sabel, C. and Zeitlin, J. (2007) 'Learning from Difference: The New Architecture of Experimentalist Governance in the EU'. *European Governance Papers (EUROGOV)*, no. C7-02 <http://www.connex-network.org/eurogov/pdf/egp-connex-C-07-02.pdf> (forthcoming in the *European Law Journal*).

SBOV (2004) *Vlaanderen en/in Europa: Omgaan met de Unie en Vergelijkend Leren*. Brugge: Die Keure.

Scharpf, F.W. (1994) 'Community and Autonomy: Multi-level policy-making in the European Union'. *Journal of European Public Policy*, vol. 1, no. 2, pp. 219-242.

Scharpf, F.W. (1997) *Games Real Actors Play: Actor-Centered Institutionalism in Policy Research*. Boulder: Westview Press.

Scharpf, F.W. (1999) *Governing in Europe: Effective and Democratic?*. Oxford: Oxford University Press.

Scharpf, F.W. (2001) 'Notes Towards a Theory of Multi-level Governing in Europe'. *Scandinavian Political Studies*, vol. 24, no. 1, pp 1-26.

Schendelen, M.P.C.M. van (ed.) (1998). *National Public and Private EC Lobbying*. Aldershot: Dartmouth.

Schendelen, R. van, and Scully, R. (eds.) (2003) *The Unseen Hand: Unelected EU Legislators*. London: Cass.

Schmidt, S.K. (2000). 'Only an Agenda Setter? The European Commission's Power over the Council of Ministers'. *European Union Politics*, vol. 1, no. 1, pp. 37-61

Schneider, G. and Baltz, K. (2005) 'Domesticated Eurocrats: Bureaucratic

Discretion in the Legislative Pre-Negotiations of the European Union'. *Acta Politica*, vol. 40, no. 1, pp. 1-27.

Shepsle K.A. (1992) 'Bureaucratic Drift, Coalitional Drift, and Time Consistency: A Comment on Macey'. *Journal of Law, Economics, and Organization*, vol. 8, no. 1, pp. 111-118.

Slaughter, A.M. (2000) 'Governing the Global Economy through Government Networks', in: M. Byers (ed.), *The Role of Law in International Politics: Essays in International Relations and International Law*. Oxford: Oxford University Press, pp. 177-205.

Slaughter, A.M. (2004) *A New World Order*. Princeton: Princeton University Press.

Soetendorp, B. and Andeweg, R.B. (2001) 'Dual Loyalties: The Boundary Role of the Dutch Permanent Representation to the European Union', in: H. Kassim, A. Menon, B.G. Peters and V. Wright (eds.), *The National Co-ordination of EU Policy: The European Level*. Oxford: Oxford University Press, pp. 211-229.

Soetendorp, B. and Hanf, K.W. (1998) 'The Netherlands: Growing Doubts of a Loyal Member', in: K.W. Hanf and B. Soetendorp (eds.), *Adapting to European Integration: Small States and the European Union*. London: Longman, pp. 36-51.

Steunenberg, B. (2006) 'Turning Swift Policy-Making into Deadlock and Delay: National Policy Co-ordination and the Transposition of EU Directives'. *European Union Politics*, vol. 7, no. 3, pp. 293-319.

Sundelius, B. and Ekengren, M. (2004) 'National Foreign Policy Co-ordination', in: W. Carlsnaes, H. Sjursen and B. White (eds.), *Contemporary European Foreign Policy*. London: Sage.

Suvarierol, S. (2007) 'Beyond the Myth of Nationality: A Study on the Networks of European Commission Officials'. Dissertation, Utrecht University. Delft: Eburon.

Talbott, S. (1997) 'Globalisation and Diplomacy: A Practitioner's Perspective'. *Foreign Policy*, no. 108, pp. 68-83.

Thedvall, R. (2006) *Eurocrats at Work* (Stockholm Studies in Social Anthropology, 58). Stockholm: Almund and Wiksell.

Thedvall, R. (2007) 'The EU's Nomads: National Eurocrats and European policy-making', in: R.A.W. Rhodes, P. 't Hart and M. Noordegraaf (eds.), *Observing Government Elites: Up Close and Personal*. Houndmills Basingstoke: Palgrave Macmillan, pp. 160-179.

Thomson, R., Stokman, F.N., Achen, C.H. and Koenig, T. (eds.) (2006) *The European Union Decides: Testing Theories of European Decision-Making*.

Cambridge: Cambridge University Press.

Trondal, J. (2001) 'The "Parallel Administration" of the European Commission National Officials in European Clothes?'. *ARENA Working Paper*, no. 25.

Trondal, J. (2002) 'Beyond the EU Membership/Non-Membership Dichotomy? Supranational Identities Among National EU Decision-Makers'. *Journal of European Public Policy*, vol. 9, no. 3, pp. 468-487.

Trondal, J. (2004) 'Political Dynamics of the Parallel Administration of the European Commission', in: A. Smith (ed.), *Politics and the European Commission: Actors, Interdependence, Legitimacy*. London: Routledge, pp.67-82.

Trondal, J. (2006a) 'Governing at the Frontier of the European Commission: The Case of Seconded National Experts'. *West European Politics*, vol. 29, no. 1, pp. 147-160.

Trondal, J. (2006b) 'An Institutional Perspective on Representation: Ambiguous Representation in the European Commission'. *European Integration online Papers* (EIoP), vol. 10, no. 4. * available at http://eiop.or.at/eiop/index.php/eiop/article/view/2006_00ma

Trondal, J. and Veggeland, F. (2003) 'Access, Voice and Loyalty: The Representation of Domestic Civil Servants in EU Committees'. *Journal of European Public Policy*, vol. 10, no. 1, pp. 59-77.

Tsebelis, G. (1990) *Nested Games: Rational Choice in Comparative Politics*. Berkeley: University of California Press.

Tsebelis, G. and Garrett, G. (2000) 'Legislative Politics in the European Union'. *European Union Politics*, vol. 1, no. 1, pp. 9-36.

Tsebelis, G. and Garrett, G. (2001) 'The Institutional Determinants of Intergovernmentalism and Supranationalism in the EU'. *International Organisation*, vol. 55, no. 2, pp. 357-390.

Wessels, W. (1997) 'An Ever Closer Fusion? A Dynamic Macropolitical View on Integration Processes'. *Journal of Common Market Studies*, vol. 35, no. 2, pp. 267-299.

Wessels, W. and Rometsch, D. (1996) 'Conclusion: European Union and National Institutions', in: D. Rometsch and W. Wessels (eds.), *The European Union and Member States: Towards Institutional Fusion?*. Manchester: Manchester University Press, pp. 328-365.

Woll, C. (2006), 'Lobbying in the European Union: From *Sui Generis* to a Comparative Perspective'. *Journal of European Public Policy*, vol. 13, no. 3, pp. 456-469.

Zwaan, J. de (2005) *De EZ Coördinatie van BZ: Goed, Beter, Best*. The Hague: Ministry of Foreign Affairs (unpublished advisory report).

ABOUT THE AUTHORS

Karin Geuijen is a postdoctoral fellow at the Faculty of Organisation, Culture and Management of the VU University, Amsterdam, and teaches public administration at the Utrecht School of Governance, Utrecht University

Paul 't Hart is professor of Political Science at the Research School of Social Sciences, Australian National University, and professor of Public Administration at the Utrecht School of Governance, Utrecht University

Sebastiaan Princen is assistent professor of Public Administration at the Utrecht School of Governance, Utrecht University

Kutsal Yesilkagit is assistent professor of Public Administration at the Utrecht School of Governance, Utrecht University

Co-authors of individual chapters

Caspar van den Berg is research associate at the Department of Public Administration, Leiden University (chapter 5)

Ellen Mastenbroek is assistent professor of Public Administration at Radboud University Nijmegen (chapter 2)

Until late 2007, Semin Suvarierol was a research associate at the Utrecht School of Governance. She has since joined Andersson Elffers Felix (Utrecht) as a junior consultant (chapter 5)

INDEX

Activity and contact pattern – 24, 100, 131, 133, 147.

Agency – 19, 31, 64, 68, 83, 93, 112, 138.

Agencies – 18-20, 26, 28, 31, 34, 57, 109, 110, 112, 121, 130, 132, 141, 149.

Allegiance – 82, 86, 101, 105, 107, 133.

Arena – 21, 22, 24, 28, 29, 51, 52, 54, 57, 72, 77-79, 81, 83, 85, 87, 90, 99-101, 104, 116, 129, 131, 134-137, 139, 141, 143-148.

Back office – 77, 87, 90, 95, 131, 132, 134, 137, 144, 147.

Bureaucrat-diplomat – 28, 87, 89, 93, 94, 98-102, 131, 133-135, 137, 147.

Bureaucratic politics – 91, 131, 132.

Career – 16, 21, 22, 31, 32, 46-48, 63, 64, 104, 105, 111, 113, 123-125, 127, 141-143, 148.
    Career development – 24, 29, 112, 141, 142, 145.

Case study – 14, 25, 27, 28, 130, 133, 134, 142, 143, 145.

Coalition – 28, 59, 72-74, 86, 89, 99, 101, 116, 135, 136.
    Coalition formation – 28, 58, 70, 72-74, 78.

Co-decision procedure – 135.

Comitology – 52.
    Comitology committee – 13, 20, 137.

Commission expert group – 13, 32, 135.

Committee – 13, 14, 19-21, 28, 52-54, 56, 59, 68, 70-74, 79, 81, 85-87, 89, 90, 92, 95, 96, 98-101, 133, 135, 137.

Competencies – 24, 139.

Co-ordination – 13, 14, 17, 21, 24, 28, 32, 46-48, 52-55, 62, 64, 66, 71, 72, 74, 81, 89, 91, 92, 94, 97, 99-102, 109, 120, 131, 132, 134, 136, 137, 140, 142, 144, 146-148.
    Co-ordination bureaucrat – 90, 100, 101, 134, 147.
    Policy co-ordination – 17, 57, 90, 144.

Council of Ministers – 14, 54, 79, 81.

Council Working Party (and group) – 13, 20, 32, 38-41, 71, 74, 80, 135.

Deliberation – 74, 78.

Departmental co-ordinator – 28, 29, 90, 99-102, 134, 147.

Dilemma – 5, 16, 21, 23, 68, 86, 146.

Diplomacy – 15-17, 19, 22, 23, 84, 129, 130.
    Classic model – 15-19, 21.
    New model – 15, 17-19, 21, 22.

Directorates-General (DGs) – 51, 59, 62, 63, 66, 67, 69, 108, 109, 115, 118, 120.

Discretion – 22, 85, 90, 91, 136, 137, 143, 144, 158.

Dispersion index (see also Organisational embeddedness) – 42-44.

Dossier team – 144.

Dutch Permanent Representation – 26, 57, 77, 78, 80, 100, 109, 115, 116, 118.

Enlargement – 72, 108, 135.

EU institution – 14, 20, 26, 28, 54, 88, 89, 93, 97, 100, 103, 109, 115, 116, 123, 131, 134.

Eurocrat – 13, 14, 23, 27, 28, 32, 33, 36, 51, 52, 59-62, 72, 74, 77, 78, 85-87, 92-94, 97, 99-102, 130, 131, 133, 135, 136, 138, 139, 142, 144, 146, 147.

Eurocratic bulwark – 42, 44, 45, 47-49, 111, 125, 141, 148.

Eurocratic runner(s)-up – 43, 45, 47, 48, 111, 141.

European Commission – 13, 14, 20, 25, 26, 28, 29, 32, 38-41, 51-74, 77, 81, 86, 89, 93, 95-97, 99-109, 112-114, 116-122, 124-126, 132, 135, 136, 138, 147.

European governance – 13, 14, 16, 23, 26, 29, 77, 85, 99, 103, 106, 113, 125, 139, 146, 147.

European integration – 13, 129, 132, 146, 147, 149.

European Parliament (EP) – 26, 54, 67, 68, 73, 74, 89, 100.

Europeanisation – 26, 28, 31, 37, 39, 44-46, 48, 49, 51, 54, 58, 74, 85, 111, 130, 131, 133, 141, 142, 148.

Organisational Europeanisation – 48, 148.

Expert – 15, 17, 51, 56, 57, 59, 70, 84, 86, 93, 100, 105-107, 111, 113, 126, 127, 133, 137, 138.

Expert committee – 20, 56, 72, 73, 70, 133, 137.

Expert community – 85, 143.

Expert group – 13, 20, 21, 32, 56, 73, 135, 138, 145.

Expert meeting – 25, 27, 88, 130, 135, 136, 138, 139, 142.

Expertise – 15-17, 21, 22, 24, 56, 60, 62, 63, 75, 85, 100, 105, 106, 109, 113, 118, 121, 126, 127, 131, 132, 139, 142, 144.

Feedback – 52, 144.

First pillar – 26, 28, 53, 78, 86, 95, 99, 133, 135, 136.

Frontloading – 28, 58, 59, 62, 73, 74, 78, 104, 116, 118, 119, 126.

High-level meeting – 89, 135.

Home government/organisation – 103, 104, 107, 111, 112, 114, 117, 120, 121, 125, 126.

Ideal type – 19, 94, 100, 131, 132.

Implementation (see also transposition) – 13, 14, 20, 26, 32, 34, 35, 38-40, 46, 51, 52, 55, 58, 62, 67, 68, 79, 83, 96, 113, 117, 132, 134-136, 147.

Informal network – 135, 136, 143.

Information – 13, 16, 19, 24, 29, 56, 58-61, 68, 72, 78, 79, 83-85, 90, 94, 95, 98, 100, 102, 104, 108, 113, 114, 116-118, 122, 126, 135, 144.

Instruction – 22, 24, 64, 74, 90, 91, 97, 107, 118, 138, 144.

Intergovernmental – 86.

International – 13, 15-17, 19, 21-23, 26,

57, 64, 66, 77, 83, 87-92, 96-98,
101, 106, 113, 125, 129, 132, 133, 137,
142.
> International organisation – 21,
64-66, 106, 114-116, 129.
Know-how – 89, 100, 104, 113.
Know-who – 104, 113.
Leadership – 93, 142, 144, 146.
Mandate – 22, 32, 46-48, 97, 119,
143.
MEP – 89, 135.
Ministry of Agriculture – 28, 42-44,
57, 60-68, 71, 110, 111, 118, 125, 142,
145.
Ministry of Foreign Affairs – 16, 17,
19-23, 34, 42-44, 110, 111.
Ministry of Health – 43, 44, 88, 91,
110, 142, 145.
Ministry of Justice – 27, 43, 44, 78, 79,
81, 83, 87, 88, 91, 92, 110, 144, 145.
Ministry of the Interior – 25, 27, 31, 43,
44, 78, 79, 82, 88, 91, 92, 142, 144,
145.
Multilateral – 16, 17. 57, 89,
> Multilateral diplomacy – 18, 129.
> Multilateral forums – 17, 19, 89,
100, 101.
> Multilateral network links – 113.
Multinational – 84, 86, 87, 107.
National administration – 14, 22, 63,
102, 103, 106, 107, 115-117, 119, 120,
122, 126, 147.
National bureaucracy – 23, 81, 148.
National champion – 44, 45, 47, 48,
141, 148.
National interest – 21, 51, 86, 90, 116,
138.
National parliamentarian – 135.
National position – 14, 28, 52-54, 75,

87, 90, 99, 100, 118, 120, 132, 138.
Network(s) – 13, 15, 22, 29, 53, 62, 65,
66, 77, 78, 85, 87, 95-100, 104, 105,
112-114, 116, 117, 119-123, 125-127,
133, 135, 136, 139, 143, 147.
Networking – 100, 113, 116, 136.
> Networking skill – 73, 140.
New diplomats – 23, 86, 99, 130.
Organisational embeddedness (see
also dispersion index) – 29, 32, 101.
Permanent Representation – 26, 57,
59-62, 65, 74, 77, 78, 80-82, 89, 95,
100, 106, 109, 115, 116, 118, 134, 142,
147.
Police co-operation – 25, 26, 28, 77-79,
82, 83, 85, 87, 94, 96, 97, 99, 101,
102, 133-135, 142, 144.
Policy network – 78, 99, 113, 114, 125,
133, 147.
Policy sector – 26, 32, 54, 55, 113, 115,
116.
Political position – 87.
Post-national – 86, 87, 93, 97, 101.
Preparation (for EU meetings) – 79,
88-90, 100.
Pre-proposal phase – 52-54, 58, 59, 73,
74.
Professional(s) – 15, 17, 19, 23, 33, 63,
69, 83, 87, 88, 93, 96, 97, 98, 100,
103, 106, 121, 122, 126, 132, 133, 135,
136, 139.
Professionalism – 18, 131, 132.
Rank – 20, 26, 27, 74, 83, 92, 107, 111,
112, 123, 124.
Rationale – 85.
Research methods – 14, 27, 129.
Role orientation – 24, 54, 78, 93, 95,
100, 131, 133, 147.
Rule – 24, 69, 78, 84, 85, 91, 94, 95,

100-102, 107, 131, 132, 135-139, 147.
   Rules of thumb – 78, 88.
Seconded National Expert (SNE) – 25, 26, 29, 58, 59, 62, 63, 64, 66, 67, 68, 69, 70, 74, 103-127, 142, 143, 147.
Secondment – 29, 63, 64, 69, 70, 74, 103-107, 109, 111-116, 118, 120-127, 142.
Sector – 25, 55, 63, 67, 68, 99, 106, 107, 115, 116, 124, 125.
Signalling – 28, 58-62, 66, 73-75, 78, 104, 116, 117, 120, 126.
Strategic behaviour – 28, 51, 54, 57, 58, 73, 99, 116, 118.
Strategy – 28, 53-59, 62, 65, 70, 73, 74, 97, 98, 109, 117, 119, 135.
Street-level entrepreneur – 28, 92, 97, 99, 100-102, 132-135, 147.
Subnational government – 130.
Supranational – 19, 26, 29, 53, 54, 63, 65, 74, 94, 103, 104, 116, 126, 133.
Survey – 14, 20, 25, 27, 31-33, 35, 42, 44-46, 48, 49, 105, 106, 111, 114, 125, 130, 134, 140, 141, 143, 145.

Questions asked in – 25, 31, 32, 105, 106, 114.
   Sample and response rate – 25, 32, 105, 106.
Technocratic – 78.
Temporary employment/staff – 106.
Third pillar – 26, 77, 78, 81, 86, 94, 95, 97-99, 135, 136.
Top management – 100, 145, 148.
Transnational – 28, 29, 77-79, 83, 84, 87, 97, 99, 100, 113, 114, 116, 126, 132.
Transposition (see also implementation) – 32, 38-41, 52, 134.
Two-level game – 146.
Uploading – 28, 52-55, 57, 58, 62, 73, 74.
Veterinary – 25, 26, 28, 51, 57, 58, 65, 69, 71, 72, 77, 78, 99, 101, 118, 133, 135, 136, 142, 143.
Virtuous circle/spiral (of organisational Europeanisation) – 48, 49, 148.
Working group – 14, 19-21, 28, 38-41, 53, 54, 64, 71, 74, 80, 81, 84, 86, 88-92, 95, 99, 100, 135.